d/DEAF and d/DUMB

Disability Studies in Education

Susan L. Gabel and Scot Danforth
General Editors

Vol. 10

The Disability Studies in Education series is part of the Peter Lang Education list.
Every volume is peer reviewed and meets
the highest quality standards for content and production.

PETER LANG
New York • Washington, D.C./Baltimore • Bern
Frankfurt • Berlin • Brussels • Vienna • Oxford

Joseph Michael Valente

d/DEAF and d/DUMB

A Portrait of a Deaf Kid
as a Young Superhero

PETER LANG
New York • Washington, D.C./Baltimore • Bern
Frankfurt • Berlin • Brussels • Vienna • Oxford

Library of Congress Cataloging-in-Publication Data

Valente, Joseph Michael,
D/deaf and d/dumb: a portrait of a deaf kid as a young superhero / Joseph Michael Valente.
p. cm. — (Disability studies in education; v. 10)
Includes bibliographical references.
1. Deaf children. 2. Imagination. I. Title. II. Title: Deaf and dumb.
HV2391.V35   362.4'2083—dc22   2010045423
ISBN 978-1-4331-0715-3 (hardcover)
ISBN 978-1-4331-0714-6 (paperback)
ISSN 1548-7210

Bibliographic information published by **Die Deutsche Nationalbibliothek**.
Die Deutsche Nationalbibliothek lists this publication in the "Deutsche
Nationalbibliografie"; detailed bibliographic data is available
on the Internet at http://dnb.d-nb.de/.

FSC
Mixed Sources
Product group from well-managed
forests, controlled sources and
recycled wood or fiber
Cert no. SCS-COC-002464
www.fsc.org
©1996 Forest Stewardship Council

Cover design by Jarod Rosello

The paper in this book meets the guidelines for permanence and durability
of the Committee on Production Guidelines for Book Longevity
of the Council of Library Resources.

© 2011 Peter Lang Publishing, Inc., New York
29 Broadway, 18th floor, New York, NY 10006
www.peterlang.com

On the last day of elementary school in fifth grade, I walk into Mrs. Kapell's classroom feeling a mix of excitement and sadness. Summer vacation starts tomorrow and next fall I begin sixth grade in the middle school building down the road. I'm about to say good-bye to my favorite teacher, confidante and friend, Mrs. Kapell.

I've been seeing Mrs. Kapell for speech therapy five days a week since kindergarten. Whenever there was trouble, I always knew where to find her.

By the time I walk through her classroom door and she turns around to say – "Hi, Joey" – tears start to stream down my cheeks. I sob uncontrollably.

"Joey, come here," Mrs. Kapell wraps her arms around me. She's a short woman, so I can rest my head on her shoulders.

I cry some more. It dawns on me then and there that I'm about to begin the rest of my life without her close by.

As I pull away from Mrs. Kapell, I can see her face looks pained. I know she's going to miss me too.

"I'm never going to meet someone like you again, Mrs. Kapell."

She responds, "Yes, you will, Joey. Throughout life you're going to have many mentors. Some will be your mentor for a short time, others for a lifetime. Your job is to find these mentors."

"How will I know how to find them?" I ask.

Mrs. Kapell smiles wide, "When you meet truly extraordinary people, you should think about the kind of person you want to be. Each of your mentors will offer something unique to you. Then each of them becomes a part of you, and that's the person you will grow up to be."

◆ ◆ ◆

I dedicate this book to my mentors.

For Mom,
Nan,
Joan Kapell,
and Joe Tobin.

Each of you shaped the superhero I am today.

ACKNOWLEDGMENTS

Without Scot Danforth's sage editorial advice, steady support, and downright hilarious Email correspondences, this book would still be nowhere close to publication. Scot is inspiring that way.

Nancy Remy came in at the eleventh hour to do last minute copy-editing, fact checking, and to keep my eyes on the prize — getting this book off to press — despite my constant efforts to change, well, just one more thing.

My older brother, John, and younger sister, Jill, allowed me to indulge childhood memories and hang on to some that they both agreed were patently false. Siblings are good like that.

I learned the art of storytelling from John. He knows how to captivate an audience with a good yarn, humor, and dead on delivery. I spent my whole childhood watching him work the kitchen table with his stories. The kitchen table is where all relatives and family friends who passed through sat for Mom's coffee and cakes and cookies. John is the kitchen table king.

Jill is the world's greatest sister because she's a fantastic, non-judgmental listener. From her, I learned the art of how to listen not only for what people say but also for how they feel. Wilma, my nickname for her since childhood (think: Fred Flintstone screaming, "Wilma!"), has always been amazingly tuned in and responsive to how this world sometimes riles me up, or gets me down. Jill is my cheerleader.

Allison, my soul mate, sat and read version after version of this manuscript at all hours of the day and night. If at any point, while reading this book, you think I'm entertaining it's likely owing to her suggestions. If I'm charming, it's entirely because of her. Thank you Alli for helping this superhero soar.

Finally, I want to thank all the folks that have been a part of this book and story — thank you for accompanying me on this journey that is my life.

TABLE OF CONTENTS

INTRODUCTION

There is no instruction manual on how to be deaf. Despite the lore shared among some American deaf people that one can go to Gallaudet University (the world's only liberal arts college for deaf and hard of hearing people) in order to earn not just a regular college degree but also to earn one's "HBD"—"how to be deaf" degree—there still is no instruction manual on how to be deaf. This lack of clear package instructions for the ontological baking of one's deaf cake is especially the case here in the post-IDEA and ADA milieu, in the age of "mainstreaming" and "inclusion" of deaf children, in the relatively new development of a global deaf "community," in the technological tide that has now so profoundly changed deaf people's access to information and social circulation, and even in the widespread popularity of American Sign Language (on both deaf and hearing hands). Deaf identities, it seems, are always already "in the making" (as Norwegian scholar Jan-Kare Breivik points out in case studies of 10 deaf people forming their identity and empowerment in a dominant hearing world through translocal and transnational frameworks). There are now, locally and globally, "many ways to be deaf," claims another book title in sociolinguistic study of international variation in deaf communities, and any "lens on deaf identities," as deaf psychologist and scholar Irene Leigh argues in her recent book of that title, will require a more or less kaleidoscopic view.

And most of the time—in these multiple makings, ways, and lenses—deaf identities here in the late 20th and early 21st century will fall between many cracks. "Stuck between" or in "betweenity" marks the toggling space I have suggested for my own deaf identity and that of many others I've come to know these days who are deaf...or Deaf...or hard of hearing...or hearing-impaired...or selectively hearing...or...go ahead, you fill in the blanks. But now, when asked to elaborate or illustrate what I might mean by this "betweenity," I don't just have to hold up the mirror, but I can also just hold up Joe Valente's memoir, point, and smile.

A big smile.

In both style and substance, form and content, Valente paints and blends for us a between space. He begins in a scene of urgent action, setting us down in the life of a young boy on the run—literally and figuratively—and for the rest of the story we will return, again and again, to this sense of perpetual animation while we also come to rest (but momentarily) in moments of Valente's suspended analysis. We are always immersed in details in this story—told by just the sort of "deaf eyes" that are typically keen on detail—and these details help place us, successfully set us down directly into scenes. Yet the details also keep us moving; they often spin and speed toward us with unsettling density, much as if we were onboard the Star Trek Voyager and had just been whipped into warp speed. Valente means for us, I think, to be in this vertigo. It is deaf space.

Inside this constantly moving narrative, the reader could essentially read one chapter plucked at random and then read another...and the connection and flow of the narrative would still be apparent. The reader can easily toggle between any and all of the chapters. Valente's imagination pulls together a not necessarily sequential or chronological tale but rather creates a kaleidoscopic story where colorful and interesting elements are all there together in his life (tube), but we, the readers, get to hold it up to the light, jog it a little, and watch for ourselves how the pieces form interesting patterns. And then we can bump it again. Our own imaginations are sparked by the imaginative turns in Valente's storytelling space.

Valente also toggles identity in this space. He is variously a "hearing person who can't hear," as one dinner companion calls him in a Phoenix restaurant, and yet he also claims attitudes, experiences, and beliefs often accorded to "Big-D" Deaf identity. He "goes native" while visiting with Ben Bahan, a well-known Deaf leader, storyteller, and professor at Gallaudet University; yet he also remains foreign, as when a young deaf preschooler at the Arizona State Schools for the Deaf and Blind teaches him what he believes is the sign for *dog*—which he then proudly performs for others—only to discover that he has been tricked and taught the sign for *tiger*. He is student and teacher at once. He is often immersed in scenes with others, yet alone. He is often alone yet immersed in active imagination. He both struggles with, and yet is also empowered by, language—sign language, spoken English, written English. He is both storyteller and critic, narrator and researcher. And he is, as one of my students pointed out after hearing Valente read selections from his book, a seeming paradox—the "suicidal superhero."

While this book was in production, Valente visited my campus to give a reading and a workshop. Over 300 people filled the auditorium, taking up all the available seats and then lining up on the stairs and clustering on the linoleum floor of a large lecture hall. Those in attendance were predominately students in our (wildly successful) American Sign Language courses but also some members of the central Ohio deaf community as well as students from my senior capstone course on "Deaf-World: Global, National, and Local Perspectives." Valente captivated the audience, pacing back and forth as he read to them with masterful delivery skills. (Mrs. Kapell, his childhood speech therapist, would surely be proud!) He was a tiger at tale-telling. In the engaged questions and discussion that followed he further offered them complex yet direct, conflicted yet confident, serious yet humorous, honest yet "I'm-making-it-all-up-as-I-go" answers. They were impressed.

In follow-up comments they said, in fact, that "it was a completely unifying experience because his stories related to everyone" and called him "good at the self-deprecating humor he writes with." They also "appreciated his sincerity" and commended "the raw, explicit tone of his writing that communicates a sense of understanding and relation that is more easily accessible to people of our age group." In sum, there were many big smiles.

Yet many of them also found it "interesting" or even "puzzling" when Valente discussed his (lack of) skills in American Sign Language. Immersed in ASL courses themselves, these students had obviously already come largely to believe (in yet another myth about deaf people) that all deaf people—especially those with "Big-D" Deaf attitudes and ideas—were skilled sign language users. One student summarized well how "new" that perspective was to them:

It was interesting when Joe Valente decided to stop being "politically correct" and told us that he wished he had been sent to a Deaf school as a child, and encouraged all parents to consider it. He then went on to describe how he knew barely any sign language, but still considered himself part of "Big-D" Deaf culture. It was the first time I had ever heard a non-signer say this.

Well, Valente has not only said that, but he has written it—in English—in this powerful book. Words are superpowers, the young Joe Valente discovers (ironically, too, not in his English class or from his English teacher, but rather from his speech therapist), and through writing, he has indeed then become a superhero. In a book on the "performance of self in student writing," Thomas Newkirk claims that "writing is always the hero of writing." There is perhaps no better poster child for that quip than Joe Valente.

Welcome then to "Joe Culture"—a culture *neither* but *also*, *and* but *or*—a culture made up of immense and intense imagination, illustrating deaf identity in the making, and told by a superhero who is sometimes closeted yet fearlessly flying through both deaf and hearing spaces.

Brenda Jo Brueggemann
Ohio State University

ONE

The Bottle Rocket Wars and Superhero Birthday

Everybody runs for cover when they hear the snap-crackle-pop from the shotgun round go off. I can feel the bullet whiz past my left ear. It makes my hearing aid whistle.

Snap. Crackle. Pop.

Whistle.

I push, I *will* my Puma sneakers to go faster. I think: I'm only eight; I'm way too young to die. I see kids making a mad dash across the aerodrome, some running to the fence, some jumping the fence, some standing safe on the other side of the fence. I can hear voices, screaming:

Run, run!

Why're they shooting us?

They're coming! Go! Go! Go!

I run. The red cape draped around my neck flies into my face. I push the cape away to look at the airport security pickup truck chasing behind. Its windshield is caked with dried mud so I can't make out the driver. I spot two men in the truck bed. They aim their single-barrel shotguns, ready their footing, and shoot.

Snap. Crackle. Pop. Snap. Crackle. Pop.

Whistle. Whistle.

I don't look back this time. I look ahead to the kids running across the dirt landing strip. Looking sideways, I see the truck pull up next to me. The security guards wear brown uniform shirts and blue jeans. They scream, Stop or we'll shoot!

The truck's front tire hits a hole hard and slams to a stop. A dust cloud rolls over the airfield. When I come out of the cloud, I see most of the kids already jumped over the fence to safety, except for me and this older, heavy kid everybody calls Fat Albert. I can hear kids near the fence mock and cheer us:

Fat Albert, go! Deaf kid, go!

Fat Albert is just ahead of me. He turns his head around and yells, It's a salt shotgun. It won't kill you, but that shit burns. Run! Run!

More bullets whistle by. We run.

The truck guns for us. My eyes watch in disbelief as Fat Albert trips over his feet. He flies into an arc through the air and belly flops to a landing just ahead of me. I can see the shadow of the truck growing larger as it closes in on us from behind.

So I shout downwind to Fat Albert lying on the ground, Your hand!

Reaching down, I lock his hand into mine, and pull him up to a racing start. I watch Fat Albert's longer legs move him fast ahead of me. When he hops up onto the fence, his shorts hook on the barbed wire. He hesitates but jumps anyway, landing on the other side of the fence with only his tighty-whiteys on.

I run full speed ahead and pull off my cape, throwing it up onto the barbed wired fence. In one motion, I jam my right foot into the chain-link fence and vault over to safety. The security truck skids to a stop on the other side.

The two men jump from the pickup bed to the ground. But the driver doesn't get out. I stand there and eye my bright red cape hanging in the barbed wire. The guards don't say anything, just smirk. Their eyes dare me to try to get it.

Fat Albert comes over and stands next to me. He says, F'git it. Not like yuh lost yur shorts.

We both chuckle. A small circle of kids gather around us, everybody laughs. I stop laughing when I see the security guards move toward the fence where my cape hangs.

I *need* my cape.

One of the security guards pulls up real close to the fence. I worry he'll try to reach for my cape up on the barbed wire now that the wind has it pinned on his side. But he only yells at us, Stop shooting bottle rockets at each other on the airfield. Got it? You're trespassing, pals. Now stay out! Next time, we call the police. Capiche?

Both of the guards hop back onto the truck bed and they speed off. I'm so happy they didn't take my cape. I'm about to go get it when a few of the older kids push through the circle, walking toward me and Fat Albert. But I stop when I see a familiar face. It's Commander, the oldest and meanest kid, the leader of the Bottle Rocket Wars. He stares down Fat Albert like he's disgusted. Commander points at him, laughs out loud, saying, Ah, looky here, Fat Albert has a brown stain on his tighty-whiteys!

Everybody looks. Fat Albert barks back to Commander, Shut up!

All goes quiet. A few kids snicker. Then everybody starts to laugh. I don't laugh. I just want to get my cape and go home.

Fat Albert gives everybody the middle finger, says, Screw you. He takes off through the woods.

With Fat Albert gone, Commander turns his attention to me. Everybody watches Commander. He leans over me some, pokes me in the chest, asks, Why yu heer?

Dunno, I say. I'm not really sure what he's asking me. I don't want to make him mad.

My answer seems to anger him, his nostrils flare. He mimics my voice with a slow-moving tongue to make me sound stupid:

Duh-nnah-nowwa

Duh-nnah-nowwa

Duh-nnah-nowwa

He keeps saying it over and over again. Everybody laughs. Finally Commander stops laughing and looks at me with a mean face. Everybody watches.

He says, Why yu dink yu ka hang out wid us? Who sez yu ka play Bottle Rocket Wars?

I'm scared. I just want to leave now. I'll get my cape later. I mumble, No 'un. Can I leave?

Commander moves in close, nose to nose, shouts, No, stay, I wanna punch yu!

Everybody moves backwards a few steps.

I pee my pants. Put up my fists to fight. Someone hollers out, Hey, look! He peed his pants! Deaf kid peed his pants!

Commander looks down at me, points at my pants, and smiles wide. He bursts out laughing and everybody else joins in.

I clench my fists, shout at everybody, Stop makin from of me!

Commander looks at the crowd and lifts his arms high in the air, pretending he's a musical conductor and they are his chorus. The mob mocks me, singing:

Stop makin *from* of me!

Stop makin *from* of me!

Commander doubles over in laughter, he's visibly pleased with his chorus. I spot an opening in the circle and take off running. I run all the way down the street to my house.

When I get home, I sneak through the door quietly. I'm relieved Mom is on the phone in the kitchen. She'd want to know why I'm not wearing my red shirt. I walk around the corner quick, go into my room, and close the door. Mom doesn't see me. I hurry to put on a clean shirt, dump the dirty underwear for clean ones, and pull on fresh pants. I bundle my pee-drenched underwear and pants into a ball and toss them under my bed near the back wall. When I step out of the room, I tiptoe softly through the short hallway into the bathroom, lock the door, and wash the dust off my face, making sure I scrub the urine off my legs with warm, soapy water. I spray my new underwear and pants with some cologne, do a once-over in the mirror, and walk out into the kitchen. Mom's still on the phone. I'm guessing she's talking with Nanny.

She hangs up and looks down at me, says, Joey, were you shooting off those firecrackers at the airport, again?

Nah, why? I kick my feet around some, not looking Mom in the eyes. I start to worry the security guards had called.

Were you? She says with a testy voice.

Nah, my eyes dart around the room and I spot cake batter in a bowl. Is that my birthday cake? I ask.

Nice try, she sounds annoyed, Joey, why is there a bottle rocket sticking out of your sneaker?

I panic. Hu, what're yu...

I go quiet and look down at my sneakers. I see the bottle rocket. It's lodged into the sole of my Pumas.

Joey, I've told you, you can't hang out with those older kids no more. They're going to get you in trouble. Now go wash up. We're going to church in a bit. And, Nanny and Poppy are coming over for your birthday party after. So go change that dirty shirt. Change those shoes. Wash that face. And, while you're at it, change your underwear – whew, something stinks like urine and perfume. What *is* that God-awful smell? When *was* the last time you changed those underpants?

She doesn't wait for an answer.

Hurry up, now, Mom says.

She says nothing about punishment. That means this talk is not over. I don't tell her I already washed up and changed my underwear. So I go sit on the toilet in the bathroom. I sit there and read Mom's *Redbook* magazine. When I come out, Mom loads me, my baby sister, Jill and older brother, John into the car for 5 o'clock mass

at Our Lady of the Snow. It's a quiet ride because we all know church is boring and
Mom likes boring. But that doesn't stop John from making his funny, goofball faces at
me. He wants to make me giggle and break the silence. That way, I'm the
troublemaker. John makes faces the whole way to church, during mass behind Mom's
back, and on the car ride home. Mom's too busy talking to the windshield in the car
and God in church. She doesn't catch on that John is clowning around.

When we pull up into the driveway, Mom tells John and me to 'disappear' until
Nanny and Poppy come and she calls on us to eat cake. I go straight to my bedroom
and close the door behind me. From my pocket, I pull out a gold key and unlock my
closet door. I get inside the closet and curl up in my dark, secret hiding place. Beside
me are some crumpled comic books, an orange plastic flashlight, a linty blue blanket,
and a black Bible I'd stolen from the church pew a few weeks ago. The comic books
remind me that I forgot my cape. I *need* my cape. I'll get it first thing tomorrow
morning, before Mom wakes up and gets Sunday bagels.

I sit in the closet and pull the blanket over my head. Shining the flashlight from
the comic books to the Bible and back again, I'm unsure what to look at first. I pick
up the Bible, it feels heavy. I judge how thick it is and rub my fingers over the raised
words: King James and Holy Bible. Thumbing through the pages, I notice it doesn't
have any pictures. I'm about to lose interest. But at random, I open the Bible and see
the name Moses. I know something about Moses from Mrs. Murphy's religion class
and a show on television.

Curious, I look at a few sentences at the bottom of the page. It reads: And Moses
said unto the LORD, O my Lord, I am not eloquent...but I am slow of speech, and
of a slow tongue.

I'm not sure what 'eloquent' means. Sounds fancy.

My mind wonders: Is Moses deaf like me? Can I be like Moses? Is Moses a
superhero? Can I have superpowers too? My imagination wanders: Like Moses, like
Spiderman, or Superman, I too have a mission in life. I will be a Saver. Father Michael
always talks about the Saver, so I'll be one too. Moses saves the Jews; Spiderman
saves Mary Jane; Superman saves Lois Lane. I'm going to be a superhero with
superpowers like them. I'm going to fight against evil like Commander. This is my
destiny.

I can't stop obsessing about becoming a superhero. My whole birthday weekend
I'm consumed with trying to figure out what superpowers to wish for. So I refuse to
blow out my birthday cake candles, telling Mom we have to wait until I can come up
with the right wish. When I say this, everybody at the table looks at me like I'm
weird. My brother, John just blurts it out, Yur weird.

Mom shoots The Look at John. Saturday night and Sunday speeds by with cake,
candy, new toys, visits from Nanny and Poppy, and hopes for a super-secret birthday
wish – what *will* my superhero powers be?

Monday morning comes quickly. For my first class, I go to speech therapy. I'm
sitting across a table from my favorite teacher and second-mom, Mrs. Kapell. She
reads a story aloud to me from *Newsday*. It's about a car crash. At the end, she asks,

What would you tell the judge if you were one of the drivers?

I would tell him that the other drive hit me first, I answer.

Mrs. Kapell wears a teasing, inquisitive face as she watches me carefully. This is my cue she's going to tease something out of me. She volleys, What do you think is the difference between saying the other driver 'bumped' or the other driver 'crashed' into you?

A courtroom and a principal's office quickly comes to mind. How much they are the same strikes me right then and there. It's the bolt that charges a connection: words are power. *Words* are superpowers.

I start grasping how words can help me. I can defend myself when I'm in trouble, and I can come up with comebacks when kids tease me. I'm miserable at this now. I can make those villains pay, I can write superhero stories about fighting them too.

Mrs. Kapell watches me. She doesn't interrupt my thinking. I look up at her, smiling and ready with an answer, I would say he crashed into me!

She laughs. Why?

Because they wuld get into more trouble!

I'm so excited. My love affair with words begins that minute. I have such an urge to write a story. Mrs. Kapell offers her teacher desk, and hands me a lined sheet of paper stapled to a green piece of construction paper to make a fancy border. The writer in me unleashes at her desk.

The green color inspires my first story named "Fluffy Mint Green Grass" about a superhero boy who dives into his lawn to time travel. Mrs. Kapell is so pleased with my story. She announces proudly, You are a wonderful writer!

She puts it in my backpack and tells me to show Mom first thing when I get home. After school lets out, I walk the block from Sylvan Avenue Elementary School, passing the sign that reads 'Deaf Child Area', and on down the street toward my house. When I arrive home, Mom as usual is waiting at the end of the driveway. Mom is pretending that she's looking in the mailbox. But I know she's looking down the street to see if I'm coming. She worries about the cars. Sometimes I can't hear them coming.

Mom walks up to give me a kiss. I hate when she does it in public so I turn my cheek away. I take out my story from my backpack to show her. She takes it and I ramble on about the story and Mrs. Kapell. By the time we reach the door to our house, she finishes the last lines, looks down at me and beams a big smile. Mom walks to the fridge and posts the story onto it with a round brown magnet. It occurs to me that it's the first time something other than a picture hangs there. She pulls my chin to look up at her, says, You're going to be a writer, Joey.

That's when knew I had found my wish. There were two wishes, in fact. Every birthday after that, I wished to be a superhero and a writer.

TWO

"Oh my God, that got to you, too!"

It's Thursday, March 15, 2007, Dr. Joe Tobin and I have driven down to Tucson from Phoenix to visit the Arizona State Schools for the Deaf and Blind. Our hope is that this might become a site where I can conduct ethnographic fieldwork on contemporary issues in the early education of deaf children. After a short wait in the lobby, a secretary leads us to the back of the building where the preschool's director, Catherine Creamer, is waiting. Catherine greets us in her office that she shares with support staff, separated by a cubicle wall. She wears a warm smile and looks curiously at us, pulling two chairs up to a table near her desk and inviting us to sit. We do the cursory introductions, explaining that I'm a doctoral student from Arizona State University and Joe Tobin is my advisor. A staff member walks past us with a child in hand, disappearing behind the cubicle. Catherine asks me "What brings you here?"

"I want to study the enculturation practices of children with deafness in preschools," I say, proud of myself for nailing the line I practiced so many times before this meeting. After the words came off my lips, though, I felt ridiculous for giving an obviously prepackaged sales pitch with academic jargon.

Joe jumps in to save me from my tendency to bore people with scholarly banter. He offers a three-minute summary of my life, accomplishments, and my uniqueness as a scholar and as a person. As Joe talks, I could see from Catherine's body language that she has latched onto something he said. She looks at me excitedly until he finishes his explanation and then asks me, "You are hard of hearing?"

"No, I am Deaf. I lip-read and hear some," I say.

Catherine looks me over and says, "I didn't know." I show her my digital hearing aid, firmly lodged in my left ear, then pointing to my right, I say, "I'm profoundly deaf in my right ear and severely hard-of-hearing in my left."

She looks at me, "Do you sign?"

I realize that now I am the interviewee.

I feel awkward, knowing the answer would take too long, I offer a quick, "Not really." I can see from her reaction that she wants to know more, so I begin telling her about my life story, growing up oral-deaf, being mainstreamed, and going from college to the doctoral program. I tell her that for a long time I have pined to be a part of Deaf culture and the American Sign Language community. I try to judge if I am going on too long, but her face shows deep interest. Catherine seems intent on figuring me out.

Then from behind the cubicle pops out a woman. "Sorry to interrupt, but I couldn't help listening to you. How did you learn to speak so well?" Catherine introduces the woman, "This is Jeanne. She works with the children one-on-one and she is a mother of two deaf children." Jeanne comes out from behind the cubicle, pulling up a chair between Catherine and myself.

Jeanne looks at me and asks again, "How did you learn to speak so well?"

I tell her the story I have told so many times before, "I was lucky. I had two great people to help me. My mom always kept me going and Joan Kapell, my speech therapist from when I was a kid, is a second-mother to me." Jeanne does not seem satisfied.

"How much can you hear?" Jeanne probes some more.

We go back and forth, as Catherine and Joe watch and listen. Jeanne wants to know more about what kind of exercises I did to practice my speech, how often I went to therapy, and what it was like to go to school. She tells me about her own children, and I start to sense that she is searching for something. It does not occur to me what that something is until much later.

After some time, Jeanne has to pull out a child for one-on-one time, so Catherine offers Joe and me a tour of the classrooms. We walk past several classrooms and look in through observation windows, while Catherine describes the preschool program and how they try to meet the needs of the range of children and their families. Most of the classes we observe appear to focus on speech, until we reach the last classroom in the hallway. Immediately, I can see the children and teachers animatedly signing to one another through the window and a friendly face, I guess to be the teacher, gestures for us to come in.

Before we enter, Catherine tells us Laurel is the last sign-only teacher at the school, that she is Deaf, and that speech should not be used in her classroom. I experience a great sense of excitement and anticipation to meet Laurel, as I fantasize she will be a like-minded radical advocate for Deaf culture and American Sign Language, a kindred spirit, albeit one who unlike me knows how to sign. As we walk through the door, Catherine, a hearing person, translates my greetings and questions to Laurel. When Laurel replies, I feel embarrassment and shame creep into me for not knowing sign. I quickly realize Laurel does not read lips. Doubly perplexed, I recognize that she does not mouth her words, so we really are without a way to communicate. I'm pained by the irony of two deaf people having to rely on a hearing person to translate.

Laurel smiles and Joe and I get down on the floor to play with the children. A young boy with dark hair, who I later learn is named, Alex, sits on Laurel's lap and signs that he wants her to read to him. I sit down next to them, and Alex nudges himself closer to me. A game ensues, where Laurel shows a picture to Alex and he responds in sign the name. I mimic the signs Alex makes and he takes the book to read with me. Laurel's attention switches to another child tugging on her arm. Alex looks to me and shows me how to say the words in sign and I model it back to him. We go through the rest of book together, and I ask if we can do it again. This time, though, I show him how quickly I can pick up the signs and make it almost to the end without needing his help. Stuck on the word "dog," Alex shows me how to make the word in sign. I proudly demonstrate to him and the rest of the class that I can now say "dog" and all the children start to giggle. Laurel's face bursts into an endearing smile, and she runs her two middle fingers down her nose to say, "Funny."

Catherine notices what is going on and explains, "Alex was tricking you, showing you the wrong word. He's teaching you tiger, not dog." We all laugh, and Alex takes my hand to read another story, but I feign as if I do not trust him now. He catches me laughing to myself, and we read a book together before I join them for circle time. He is my new buddy. I feel like I found a safe place, no worries about hearing, only signs. I'm almost euphoric with sentimentality.

After a few minutes of circle time, Catherine invites Joe and me outside and Laurel leads the class through their end-of-the-day rituals before the bus comes. After all the children go outside, Laurel joins us in conversation, with Catherine translating. I notice the afternoon students arriving and teachers greeting the children, and checking the cochlear implants that look like little black coins attached to their heads, while teachers also twist hearing aids outward to test batteries and make sure they are on. The children seem to willingly accept this practice.

Catherine asks me, "Did you ever consider a cochlear implant?"

Without thinking, I quickly respond, "Absolutely not. I'd rather not speak."

"Why?" Catherine looks puzzled and translates my words in sign for Laurel.

"Because I always thought that if and when I lost my residual hearing that I would simply use ASL," I look to Laurel for approval, looking for signs that she understands and approves of my position.

Catherine signs what I said and Laurel looks at me and then pulls her hair back on one side of her head, revealing that she, too, has a cochlear implant. I feel confusion, as my mind flashes to images of cyborgs, Frankensteinian experiments, and sci-fi movies with lines like, "Oh my God, that got to you, too!" I am unsure how to respond.

When I got over the shock and asked her why, as an ASL teacher, she got a cochlear implant, Laurel replied, "Mostly for music and dancing." Until that point, I had never considered that if and when I lose my residual hearing how my feelings against cochlear implants, and technology in general might be impacted by the reality of music disappearing from my life.

I realize now that the new world of Deaf culture is not the same one I had been reading about for so long. Deaf culture is evolving with technology, as is the rest of the world. Seeing Laurel with a cochlear implant makes me feel uneasy that the battle lines between speech and sign are less clear than I had thought. The Deaf culture I had built up in my imagination was not the same Deaf culture I was encountering on my first initiation into fieldwork at the Arizona School for the Deaf.

This first encounter with Laurel and Alex and the school set into motion a whole series of thoughts. The Deaf culture I was encountering seemed to be on the move. I now realize this romanticized version of Deaf culture that I had frozen in my mind into an idyllic time and place did not exist. To learn more about Deaf culture, I was going to have to let go of my utopian fantasy of it. With my limited view of Deaf culture, I saw myself as already part of it even though I do not even know American Sign Language. I now better appreciate that to wholly be a part of Deaf culture I really do need to know sign language. It tortures me that I do not already know how to sign, it pains me to no end to not be able to chat with my Deaf peers with ease. Being tricked by Alex, a fellow newcomer to Deaf culture, did more than make me realize that I didn't know ASL, it also made me see more clearly what it is that I wanted to get out of this project. I want to belong somewhere.

I cannot help but wonder: Where do I – this deaf kid who lives in between the Deaf and hearing worlds – where do I belong?

THREE

An Anatomy of My Journey to Deaf Culture

I start with these two stories, one from long ago and one more recent, because they each introduce central and parallel themes of this book. The first story introduces this in-between underworld I have been a part of since childhood – an imaginary world all my own. While the second is a real-world story that introduces the conflicting sentiments I felt as an oral deaf outsider with romantic visions of Deaf culture meeting Laurel, an insider who wears a cochlear implant. These two stories also provide a preview of how the chapters ahead weave my own life history and my journey still in-progress toward Deaf culture.

I aim to move along temporalities – past, present, and real-time in this narrative that is part autobiography, part autoethnography, and part autobiographical novel, with some interpolated tales inserted along the way. I self-consciously give a literary inflection to this work, drawing on conventions of two early forms of the novel, the picaresque and *bildungsroman*, to track my life as a young deaf kid to my development as a scholar and as a Deaf person up to this very moment that I am writing. I now realize that this work and this journey will never be complete.

My meeting that fateful March 15th day with Joe Tobin, Catherine (the school director) and most especially, Laurel and her preschool students energized me and challenged the way I thought about d/Deaf culture and young children. My visits and contacts with other schools for the deaf and informants across the country and around the world both encouraged and alarmed me, so much so that it led me to write these chapters in a more intimate, confessional, and critical manner than I initially planned. I first set out to write a more traditional ethnography of early schooling for the deaf. The reworking of the plan for this project evolved under the guidance of my mentor, Joe Tobin, who encouraged me to continue to blur the stylistic boundaries of storytelling and research. We both felt encouraged after the positive reception given to my presentation of some of the narrative sections of the project at the American Educational Research Association (AERA) meeting in New York City on March 26, 2008.

I began this project from the cultural anthropological perspective that preschools serve as sites of enculturation, sites that socialize young children into localized (for example, family, school, and community) and globalized (for example, state-wide, national, and international) cultural worlds. In my mind, investigating preschools for the deaf, which serve as starting sites of enculturation, would enable me to better understand the cultural worlds of deaf children. As I entered into my investigation of the connections between d/Deaf culture, young children, and schooling, the emergence of unforeseen complexities and events shifted the original foci of and organization of this study. What I ended up discovering and uncovering required me to rethink how to approach this project. I realized that this project required transparency, self-reflection, and self-critique about what was happening to me as my study was evolving as a researcher, a storyteller, and a Deaf man. This study started out as an ethnographic account of early schooling of the deaf. Instead this study morphed into an anatomy of my journey into Deaf culture.

I eventually came to the realization that I was/I am too intellectually and emotionally invested to be able or willing to perform the role of an even partly detached ethnographer. I could not distance myself from my own life history and subjectivity enough to approach and analyze these phenomena with the kind of genuine open-mindedness and curiosity and a non-judgmental stance that would be required epistemologically and ethically to conduct an ethnography of the contemporary world of deaf education. I could not listen sympathetically to parents explaining their decision to give cochlear implants to their young children or make decisions that would do anything other than provide their young children with a sign-rich environment. At this point in my life, I am simply not ready to offer any concessions to the machinations of hearing-world domination. My standpoint here is therefore in direct contradiction to the traditional role of the ethnographer who approaches a culture with some degree of objectivity and a cultural relativism that requires withholding judgment.

These chapters fuse the vernaculars of social sciences and humanities, the scientist as storyteller. James Joyce (1939) challenged dichotomies by taking the position of "one aneither" to transcend limiting, binary ways of thinking. The concept of "one aneither" inspires my methods of meshing science with story, drawing on distinct methods and writing styles as a vehicle to cross between hearing and Deaf worlds. My voice bears the accent of a researcher who uses stories, both personal and those of my informants, to investigate multiple perspectives and conflicting viewpoints on deaf and/or Deaf cultural values, young children/childhood, and schooling.

These chapters are not about Deaf or disability culture alone. Many other authors have written eloquently on these topics with far more authority than I can. My academic training is in the fields of childhood studies, educational anthropology, literature, and critical theories that seek to reconceptualize the way we think about schools, children, families, communities, research, and storytelling. I am only an expert on the topics of Deaf culture and disability in so far as my knowledge comes from personal experiences and from my learning as a self-taught Deaf and Disability studies scholar. Though I have spent the majority of my life as an oral deaf person, living, learning, and working in the hearing world, I have been reading and learning about Deaf culture and schools for the deaf for well over ten years. It all began with writings by well-known Deaf culture experts that I had aimlessly selected to read – Nora Ellen Groce, William Stokoe, Harlan Lane, John Van Cleve, as well as Carol Erting, Brenda Jo Brueggemann, Ben Bahan, Dirksen Bauman, and Paddy Ladd. I also visited the first American School for the Deaf in Connecticut, sites near Martha's Vineyard historical Deaf community in Massachusetts, Gallaudet University in Washington, D.C., and schools for the deaf throughout the United States and internationally. I have spent years reading prominent Disability studies critics including Jan Valle, Philip Ferguson, Linda Ware, Simi Linton, Lennard Davis, Thomas Skrtic, and Michael Bérubé. Each of these writers in unique ways inspired me to become the writer I am today. I read these writers for personal reasons, so I could better understand my life experiences and myself as a deaf kid and now as an adult.

It seems serendipity and good fortune has given me the opportunity to meet some of my favorite writers in person on this journey to Deaf culture. I felt especially honored to have met: Jan Valle, Philip Ferguson, and Linda Ware while serving on a panel at the AERA conference in New York City; Michael Bérubé, who so warmly welcomed me to Pennsylvania State University; Carol Erting and Dirksen Bauman, who so kindly granted my wish to present on this book at Gallaudet University; Brenda Jo Brueggemann, who gave this book the thumbs-up needed to move it along to publication and graciously agreed to write the Foreword; and finally, Ben Bahan and his lovely family – Sue, Juliana, and Davy – who all so warmly welcomed me into their home and were my guides into the DEAF-WORLD. I could never have anticipated I would be so lucky to meet some of the very people who have inspired me to become the writer I am today. Likewise I could never have known some of these very same folks would become key characters in my life story.

I never intended to enter the field of Deaf studies or Disability studies, choosing instead to stand by on the margins, thinking my experiences somehow less valid than "scientific" training. If I am an expert on anything, I am an expert on navigating and "passing" in the hearing world. I do not live fully in either the hearing or Deaf worlds. For years I thought this "in-between" world was mine alone. I have since learned this is not true.

Paddy Ladd (2003), whose work in Deaf studies has deeply moved me and inspired my work, notes that, "existence as a Deaf person is actually a process of becoming," and these accounts delve into children and adult informants' processes of *becoming* (p. 3). The journey ahead is also both personal and professional, simultaneously documenting my process of *becoming* a member of the Deaf community and *becoming* a Deaf studies and Disability studies researcher. I also unveil the process of this book's *becoming*; to be written through the eyes of one who has been personally immersed into these paradoxical worlds of hearing and Deaf.

Methods, Theoretical Lenses, and Organization

The research methods and theoretical lenses employed in the pages ahead borrow from multiple sources and across fields including anthropology, autobiography, autoethnography, Critical Race Theory, cultural studies, Cyborg theory, Queer theory, DeafCrit, Deaf studies, decolonizing methods and theories, Disability studies, life history and narratives, literary theory, narrative inquiry, post-structural/post-modern theories, sociocultural theory, indigenous/subaltern traditions, and more. Throughout my journey, I often reached to my tool belt of methods and theories to explicate unforeseen phenomena that emerged. I have been a bricoleur, of sorts, using whatever tool and materials were at hand.

I set out at the onset to use the autobiographical and autoethnological methods only briefly for the introduction of this project. After the AERA conference, I decided to move away from conducting a traditional ethnographic study to the current autobiographical, autobiographical novel, and autoethnological narrative in order to allow me the freedom and opportunity to share the unexpected phenomena that emerged and why I felt (and continue to feel) so strongly against the special and rehabilitative education establishment, the medical community and extended networks, and discourses and apparatuses that I believe oppress and subjugate children who are d/Deaf.

I decided to make my journey and me the central characters of this study and story. I chose autobiographical narrative to create a dialogic mirror. This dialogic mirror is a reflection on how I see the world and how I reconcile my past with today. In the traditions of the picaresque and of *testimonio*, my presence as the protagonist and narrator of this story is an intentional device for commenting intimately and critically on the social world I'm encountering on this journey. This is not purely a narcissistic or egoist exercise (though I recognize to some extent it is), but a way for me to give you, the reader, an opportunity to vicariously live this journey with me, with me and my life history as your guide.

This book is a multilayered research novel, traversing the fields of arts and sciences to present a portrait of my life as a "deaf kid" who becomes a "young superhero." It travels from my origin story, to the hard road from schoolchild to subaltern subject. While talking about my past memories with family and friend informants, the key theme of my alternating identity between "deaf kid" and "young superhero" takes shape. Next it builds on the ideas of superheroes, mentors, and villains to illustrate the birth of my emerging, powerful identity as a subaltern superhero fighting against the kryptonic hearing-dominated forces who crusade to "fix" me and the Deaf. The final chapters peer into my life as a "young superhero" writer today, unearthing the costs and advantages of having lived this "in-between" life: my loneliness, my pain, my super-sensitivity to those silenced, and my super-powerful storytelling. At times throughout this journey, I take diversions reminiscent of the picaresque novel and introduce comic-book-style interpolated stories (with the signature characters: Commander, Sean, Mrs. Kapell, and others). These interpolated stories slowly unmask how my own life history and alter(nating) identity drives the young superhero scholar and storyteller I am today and I will strive to be. What I learn from this journey: d/Deaf and d/Dumb is forever.

FOUR

A Hysterical Mother Without a Deaf Kid Instruction Manual

The smell of saltwater wafts along the coast of the Great South Bay and from the Atlantic beyond, where a seaside hamlet named Bayport on Long Island, New York, sits largely undisturbed by the bustling, hyper-hip megapolis fifty miles west. It's the fall of 1975, six weeks after I was born. My father works overtime close to the City. Mom is home alone with my one-year-old brother, John, and me. Before midnight, Mom notices my body temperature rising fast. She panics. Mom wakes John and sets us both down in the backseat of our family car, a red 1973 Oldsmobile Cutlass. She drives from our house on Bayport Avenue to the Brookhaven Hospital's emergency room just off Sunrise Highway, about fifteen minutes away.

The doctor diagnoses it a case of an "overreacting" mother, a "hysterical" woman. He sends us home. Shortly after getting John back to bed, she notices my forehead reaches a feverish pitch. I'm sweaty and screaming. Mom follows the doctor's orders and rubs me down with cold wet towels. She keeps compulsively rewetting towels with cool water from the sink. Then I stop screaming. Mom becomes frantic, unsure what to do. She drives me with little John in tow to the hospital in Riverhead, about thirty minutes eastbound on Sunrise Highway. Racing through farm country on a weaving, lightless two-lane road, her heart pumps with panic. She hears my breathing getting shorter. When Mom finally pulls up in front of the hospital, she grabs us from the backseat of the Cutlass and runs. Mom carries John and me in each arm and crashes through the emergency room doors.

My short life is almost over. The hospital staff admits me, hurries me away. Nurses dunk me into a tub filled with ice cubes and cold water. It brings the fatal fever down, at once rescuing me from death and baptizing me into the world of deafness. A nurse tells Mom I have double-pneumonia. The high fever almost killed me. Mom stands off to the side with John, she watches. Nurses and doctors poke and prod me. Her heart fills with pain.

The hospital staff then calls the police.

They tell the police to bring Mom up on charges of neglect and endangering the welfare of a child. Mom becomes "hysterical." She explains that this is all the fault of the emergency room doctor back at Brookhaven. Mom tells them to call the other hospital. Once they confirm our earlier visit, the doctors and police drop the threats. Some apologize. Some don't.

After a month in the hospital, I'm finally released. Everybody is uncertain what and how much of an effect the high fever had on me. Much later, around the time I'm in preschool, doctors guess it's the high fever that ravaged my inner ears, severely damaging the left side and completely deafening the right. In pseudo-clinical terms, doctors tell Mom the right ear is profoundly deaf – there is simply no sound and never will be. The left ear is diagnosed with a severe to profound sensorineural hearing loss. That means the hair cells in the left ear's cochlea so crucial for telling the difference between spoken sounds are largely dead.

In simple terms, I'm very deaf.

When most people meet me, they inevitably ask, "How deaf are you?"

I can't honestly tell where this answer comes from but my response every time without thinking is: "In my right ear, I'm 100 percent deaf, no hearing at all. In my left, I'm 95 percent deaf. With a hearing aid on, I can hear about 5 to 10 percent more. I mostly read lips."

Truly I don't know if it is true that I'm 95 percent deaf. It sounds right. I do know audiologists don't use those terms to describe my or anyone else's hearing loss.

Even after people learn this about me, it's still all touch and go. As I grew up details about my deaf condition and how to live with it in this world became clearer.

Mom would sometimes say, "You didn't come with an instruction manual."

If there were a manual, it would have saved us all what took a lifetime to learn. With a hearing aid on the left ear, I often mishear the sounds "b" for "p" and "ch" for "sh." I often mistake: motorcycles for blowing wind; ticking clocks for dripping faucets; and, a woman for a man on the phone. I also often misunderstand that people are listening when they are actually talking and a friendly voice for an angry tone. Everybody knows I can't hear with the lights off. I don't do large crowds or echoey rooms. People who talk with hands or objects in front of their mouths deserve "smile and nod" responses. Unkempt mustaches make it doubly harder to read lips. Generally I won't do water activities because I can't get my hearing aid wet.

A manual would also have to explain seating arrangements. For example, in a booth I need to sit so that my left ear can hear everyone at the table and the waiter (but likely I will ask the person next to me to repeat what the waiter said anyway). Booth conversations require a mix of listening and speech reading. At a round table, I speech read because everybody to my right is silent. If it is a rectangle-shaped table, I talk to the person next to me. The worst are classrooms with desks in rows, I don't read lips or listen, only daydream. Walking has similar challenges, except I can't watch where I'm going if walking and talking at the same time are required.

Finally a manual would have to explain that if I don't hear you, first, wait a few seconds before repeating, sometimes in the time it takes the sound to get from my hearing aid to the processing center of my brain, there exists a brief delay. Oftentimes there is some holdup in interpreting the garbled sounds I initially hear into intelligible speech.

If I still need you to repeat, please understand that I don't have an auditory loss but a sensorineural loss. That means, I don't need you to speak louder, I just need you to repeat the sounds I missed. If there were a deaf kid instruction manual, most certainly it would start with all this.

FIVE

Tropical Storms, Time Travel, and an Incomplete Baptism

Tuesday dawns hazy and humid. It's November 10, 2009, and Hurricane Ida hit the coast off the Gulf of Mexico this morning. The television tells me Ida has been downgraded to a tropical storm but warns of coastal and inland flooding as she makes her way across the Florida panhandle. I stand at the window, watching dark clouds and heavy rain move in on the city of Tallahassee, Florida. This is where I live and work now as an assistant professor at Florida State University. I'm restless and lost in thought. I've been up all night so I'm still wearing the ripped blue jeans and T-shirt I wore yesterday. I track the blue-gray clouds inching over my red brick house. A few large drops of rain come first, followed by a downpour. The rain shower starts to calm me down some. I take a seat at my desk, sit, and stare out the window. Looking out the window, my front lawn reminds me of the first story I ever wrote in Mrs. Kapell's speech class about being a superhero who time travels by jumping into fluffy mint green grass. I remember thinking as a kid how clever I thought I was for coming up with such a sensory-rich description – fluffy, mint, green grass. I think about this story often. Sometimes it's foremost in my mind for days.

If only I could go back in time. If only I could do like the superhero in my first story did and travel back in time by jumping into some fluffy mint green grass. I would go back to those days when I was younger and those mean kids or school got me down and cheer little Joey up. I would tell my younger self everything would turn out way better than I ever dreamed. I would share all the exciting things that will happen when I'm older like traveling around the world, being a writer, and a superhero. Well, not the kind of superheroes I read about in the comic books but a superhero nevertheless.

Except really, there is no fluffy mint green grass to jump into to travel back in time. There are only memories. I'm not always so certain about how true my memory recollections are but I do know one thing for sure – that is, without my imagination, I would have given up on life. I know that much.

As a kid I worried a lot about losing my imagination. I feared once I reached a certain age my imagination would expire. In the adult world I knew, there was no room for imagination. These are the things I think about often, even these days.

My eyes fix out the window on the front lawn. But now my mind's eye shifts inward. I imagine myself jumping into my lawn and into this time travel vortex. It feels as if I'm time traveling through my life with scenes beginning from my birth and on quickly replacing one another in rapid sequence. Locations from each scene of my life flash by: a red Oldsmobile Cutlass; monkey bars on a playground; a wood-paneled principal's office; the Bayport Aerodrome. I keep time traveling until, abruptly, I land somewhere around 2006 when I was a graduate student at Arizona State University. I'm in a small class of about twelve students. The class is called post-structural theory and it's taught by Dr. Joe Tobin. I remember that this is the class where Joe led a discussion on these two theorists named, Michel Foucault and Louis Althusser. I remember this day so clearly and how excited I was when the idea came to me that I could use this newfound critical lens to look at my life. I had found a way to transform painful memories into superpowerful memories. It was therapy by theory. Instead of being some "deaf kid," I was using these theorists to re-imagine my life story. I decided I wanted to imagine myself to be a "young superhero," fighting for survival under a tyrannical regime with forces of Darkness everywhere. It made me feel like my suffering had a purpose, like it had prepared me for my destiny as a superhero crimefighter. These theorists also gave me super-strength to re-envision and revisit moments in my life where I felt powerless. When I travel in time, it makes me feel as if I'm like Superman in the movie where he spins Earth backwards to reverse time after a massive earthquake. Time travel makes me feel I too can right the wrongs of the past.

I can now channel Foucault and Althusser into my thinking on command. In memories from my childhood, I can see a characteristic of Foucault's new age mind control (which forces us to police ourselves) and Althusser's portrayal of dogmatic technologies (which forces us to become obedient masses). I can see how Foucault and Althusser might view my life as a "deaf kid"-turned-"young superhero."

I think to myself: For sure, Foucault and Althusser would agree when I say the "deafing and dumbing" of children who are deaf is at its core a colossal, evil empire. The empire's web ensnares a deaf child from diagnosis and on, making for a formidable collective force. This collective force includes doctors, teachers, hearing aid and cochlear implant merchants, social workers and speech therapists. Each performs the role of cultural authority figures in a charade that calls for fixing the Deaf. All these authority figures, knowingly and/or unknowingly, belong to a complex collective of hospitals, schools, equipment providers and businesses, welfare and rehabilitative agencies, and so on. All these people and organizations together force deaf children to become patients, special education students, hearing aid or cochlear implant or speech therapy consumers, and welfare and rehabilitation dependents. These forces all start and stand to gain from the premise that deaf children need to be fixed. This need to be fixed perpetuates the endless cycle of rehabilitation. The hidden practices of what I call "deafing and dumbing" children. "Deafing and dumbing" children who are deaf manifests itself through an internalizing of this status of always needing to be fixed. What I can see more clearly now is that the way we think or do not think about deaf people drives these forces to be either helpful or harmful. Theory gave me the words to articulate how this "deafing and dumbing" happened and still happens today to both young deaf children and me.

What I know now is that how we think about the world is a living theory. It influences our perceptions, which then influences our actions. These living theories have real world consequences. They come to life in our homes, communities, and world in real ways. French historian, Michel Foucault (e.g., 1978; 1992; 1995) tells us about the transition of a powerful technology from body to mind, a form of mass mind control. Foucault provides a genealogy of this oppressive force. During the nineteenth and the twentieth centuries, these oppressive forces shifted from religious external controls and discipline of the body to mind control. But the term "mind control" is too simplistic. Foucauldian mind control is more than societal controls, it is also how knowledge itself is accepted, resisted, dismissed, even sometimes transformed. This mind control dresses itself up as unquestioned truth yet when stripped to its naked core reveals that knowledge itself is power. Those who own knowledge also own our bodies and minds. These modern internal controls police the "soul" or mind, tricking the subjects themselves into doing the dirty work of oppression. Foucault unveiled the birth of a new force to control people. This force works to control the masses more subtly and with less maintenance. The force itself is reproduced by an unsuspecting majority population – internalized and hidden. It's a force still very much alive today.

Living theories are also known as beliefs, dogmas, or ideologies. Louis Althusser (1972) writes about how people are molded into subjects by an ideology. He writes about how subjects are constructs of an ideology. For instance, how a society might construct what it means to be a patient, student, soldier, or prisoner is dependent on ideology. Each and every subject is a cultural actor, performing the role that defines who we are and what we can be. Althusser explains how each subject is a docile participant in an elusive web-like system of social institutions. He calls these social institutions ideological state apparatuses. Subjects are shaped by the workings of these ideological state apparatuses. Hospitals, schools, rehabilitation businesses, and welfare agencies are the tentacles of these ideological state apparatuses. Collectively they work to make possible the linguistic, social, and cultural violence perpetrated against deaf children and their families. The violence is evidenced on our televisions and movie screens and radio airwaves; our newspapers, magazines, scientific and educational journals, policy papers and political rhetoric. These are all part of the ideological state apparatus. Together these violent forces use discourse as a way to reproduce deficit views of deaf people. The ideological state apparatus sustains conditions of oppression against deaf children.

Conditions of oppression surround the child nonstop both from the outside and inside. On the inside, however, there is another force at work that Althusser (1972) calls interpellation. Unlike the more visible ideological state apparatus, evidence of interpellation is much trickier to unearth. Deaf children and their parents are interpellated by hearing-dominated views that have always already existed about deaf people, namely, that they need to be fixed. Parent and child are interpellated by views that reproduce conditions making them think of deafness as something that needs to be cured. These interpellated views work to normalize and reform the failing, unruly ears. Always already failing deaf children are eternal seekers of Hearingness; that is, they internalize the expectations of the "ab/normal" subject position. The end result is the reproduction of reigning hearing ideologies controlling the body and mind (Althusser, 1972). But there are those that resist these forces.

Foucault's (1992) writings on identity make clear how these powerful forces work. He demonstrates what all anti-authority struggles have in common, empowering those who resist oppression with a simple yet insightful question and response:

> Who are we? [We] are a refusal of these abstractions, of economic and ideological state violence which ignore who we are individually, and also a refusal of a scientific or administrative inquisition which determines who one is (p. 306).

Who are we? Who am I?

Who are we? Who am I? It feels strange to be writing about myself in a forum usually reserved for words that convey objective authority, language, and research. After years of learning how to conduct traditional scholarship, I now realize that life histories can be fertile ground for research and understanding my life as a "deaf kid." During a phone conversation with my mother about this project, she told me the part about the hospital calling the police that day I became deaf. I was shocked. When I asked why she never told me this before, my mother responded that I had never asked.

When I prod her to tell me more about this, my mother explains that what she wanted most was for people around her to understand. She clarifies this with an oft-repeated line: empathy, not sympathy. Most often, she tells me, the education and medical community treated her with a combination of sympathy and derision for her failings as a parent. She failed to have a normal child; she failed to listen when people set limits on me; she failed to understand that she had a disabled child. My mother's position was not political, it was not educational, nor cultural. She simply refused to accept failing. Failure was not an option with my mother. Even now, my mother refuses to acknowledge I have a disability. I'm not even deaf. It's just better, as she says, to look at me when speaking.

I should take a brief pause here to explain that when I first broached the idea of doing this memoir to my mother, she expressed concern that by telling people too much about our personal lives we risked being judged. She worried about the costs of doing and sharing this work with readers. My mother didn't say it, but I knew she felt she wanted to be done with being judged as a mother. I could certainly understand her concerns and her desire for some privacy and peace. She also worried we might step on old wounds, even if only by accident. I assured her we could handle it.

We both agreed at the outset of this project there were a few areas that would be off-limits for this book. Actually each of us picked one area. My mother chose any topic related to my absent, abusive, and alcoholic biological father (and later added a few smaller, insignificant – in terms of my life story growing up deaf – off-limit topics). I seconded her and also chose the multiple surgeries to treat my "skin cancer." Each of these topics were outside the bounds of our comfort zones. Mostly, I can only speak for myself here, because these wounds have yet to heal. As of now, I'm simply not ready to talk or write too much more about either my biological father or the cancer scare. This is why this book is a portrait of my life as a deaf kid, not a memoir. Believe me, there is still much to tell.

In conversations with my mother, she shares with me feelings of being a failing parent, fears of being constantly judged by professionals, and doubts she had about what was best for me. For her, it all started on that day in those hospitals, continuing as she advocated for me to be able to attend public schools and be mainstreamed. For me, it all started when I went to preschool and continues even to this day.

With Foucault and Althusser in mind, I now have a different view of my first hospital stay and my years in school. I can easily summon memories of my early life. But making these familiar memories strange has been a tougher task. I have been compelled to think about these and other thought-provoking questions throughout my investigations of preschools for the deaf across the country. My preschool parent, teacher, and staff informants often ask me: Why do I want to study young children with deafness, their families, and preschools? My simple answer: I want to give *life* to stories like and unlike my own about growing up with deafness in a hearing-dominated world. *Life*, not *voice*. *Voice* implies speech is necessary for empowering people, whereas *life* recognizes the visual culture of deafness and shows deference to *lived experiences*, frequently overlooked in research on deafness and disabilities in general.

I usually find that my simple answer leads to more questions. My informants repeatedly turn the tables and ask me questions: How come I never learned sign language? What schools did I go to? How did I learn to speak so well? How have I been so successful in the hearing world? What do I recommend for their child? Everyone has a different angle they want to explore, reinforce, validate, or understand. I am always ambivalent about these questions, fearful to become a poster-boy for speech-only advocates or to make recommendations for what course to follow. Though communication-wise I am *oral deaf*, I feel that I am *culturally Deaf*. I am never sure how much about myself and my beliefs and perspectives to reveal.

This book is a departure from this personal history of reticence. First through Foucauldian and Althusserian lenses, I recount selected episodes from my own experiences as a special education student and lone "deaf kid" in mainstream public school, where feelings of alienation, stigma, and internalized failure continuously competed with feelings of acceptance, pride, and possibility. After each memory reconstruction and informant interview, I use the "self as instrument" to (re)discover how my personal history shapes who I am as a researcher and storyteller (Eisner, 1991; Clandinin and Connelly, 2000; Barone, 2001).

Throughout this journey I also examine the usage of "d/Deaf and d/Dumb," influenced by the tradition of subaltern (e.g., Said, 1993; Spivak, 1988) and indigenous decolonizing (Smith, 1999) tactics, as a way of renaming and reconceptualizing stories of physical versus cultural deafness along with silence versus empowerment (Ladd, 2003, 2005). With historical roots that can be traced back to Aristotle, the term "deaf and dumb" has been used to indicate a lack of voice and, by extension, intellect. The term "d/Deaf" refers to a bicultural English/American Sign Language lifeworld and also to conceptions of physical versus cultural deafness (Woodward, 1972). More recently, "d/Deaf" has been used to portray the space between the identities of those living in the hearing and Deaf-Worlds (Baynton, 1996; Senghas and Monaghan, 2002). I make a parallel move by introducing the term "d/Dumb," using the small "d" in "dumb" to refer to the historical silencing of those with deafness (Padden and Humphries, 2005) and the big "D" version to rename the term by recognizing its painful historical lineage and to indicate the space (and struggles) between silence and empowerment that inevitably are the realities of children with deafness who navigate their way in a hearing-dominated world.

Ethicists concerned with the often cloaked relationship between power and knowledge suggest, "one could say that power relations have been progressively governmentalized, that is to say, elaborated, rationalized, and centralized in the form of, or under the auspices of, state institutions" (Foucault, 1992, p. 317). Internalized hegemonic (pre)conceptions of deafness "by its very 'common senseness' is hard to recognize, harder to change" (Thoryk, Roberts and Battistone, 2001, p. 188). H-Dirksen Bauman (2004) argues that the unquestioned phonocentric "position has become a part of hearing-centered 'common sense.' Deaf people come into contact with audist attitudes, judgments that mask oppressive ideologies" (p. 240). Harlan Lane (2002) notes, "I asked a colleague, a university professor I'll call Archibald, whether he thought that Deaf people have a disability. 'Of course they do,' he answered, 'it's common sense'" (p. 356).

By examining my own life history, this book problematizes "common sense" approaches to raising and educating young deaf children. It also unearths the subtle patterns of governing the deaf body (e.g., Foucault 1992, 1995; Baker, 2002, 2003; Padden and Humphries, 2005). These governing patterns are reflective of an audist epistemological and normative ideological position, where deafness is regarded as a deficit to be rehabilitated and children are to be (mis)educated (Lane, 2002, 2005; Ladd, 2003, 2005).

Even now, my baptism into the Deaf-World is unfinished. Linguistically I am still an outsider. Claiming my "Deaf" identity has been a long and challenging journey. Claiming my colonized-self and unlearning my "deafness" has been and remains to be an even harder task. I am thirty-four years of age and I can look back on my life and clearly see the trajectory of my coming out Deaf (Linton, 1998; Ladd, 2003, 2005). This incomplete baptism – this journey has been both exciting and painful. I've lived all my life in an imaginary place I created all my own that is bordered by the Deaf-World and the majority Hearing-World. Sometimes, I desperately wish I could have lived in one location or the other, anywhere, but in-between.

SIX

Old Sparky and Grammas' Sweet Shoppe and Ice Cream Parlor

The first shock comes straight from the leather headstrap contraption buckled onto my chin. It sends a bolt of electricity to the center of my skull. I can feel the electric shock pierce both my eardrums. An aftershock jerks my cranium rearward with a quick jab-cross-hook combination. Old Sparky is abuzz.

I can feel this first jolt tremor the length of my vertebrae to the sternum, over the ribcage, around the hips, and on downward through to the femur, tibia, and fibula, fizzling off finally at the toes. With my arms pinned down, my body slumps forward some in the electric chair. Twice more the electric shocks come.

Jab-cross-hook.

Jab-cross-hook.

Fizzle. Fizzle.

When I come to, I lift up my head a bit and open my hard boiled eyes. I can make out what seems to be the color red. It comes into focus some more. I can see it is my cape. I *need* my cape.

The cape lies over an office chair, just outside the chamber beyond the thick glass where a crowd of white-coat, doctor-types now stand. They have their backs turned to me. I'm guessing they were here to witness the execution. Little do they know, I have superpowers and I *can't* die. I'm a superhero.

I drop my head and chin into my chest. I fake I'm dead. Everything is silent inside the chamber. I don't hear anything outside it either. A few minutes go by, then some more. No one comes in to check on me. I keep waiting. To make it appear like I died, I keep myself stock-still, slow my breathing down, and imagine rigor mortis setting in. I let some drool trickle outside the side of my mouth, down my cheek, and off my chin onto my shirt. I heard once on a TV show that when people died they pooped and peed themselves. I didn't want to do that so I force a fart. The smell lingers a bit in the stale chamber air until finally the door creaks open. I clench my eyes real tight. Play dead. The doctor-types come into the chamber of death.

I hear a silent voice, Goodness, whew, then a slow whisper, *Th-th-a-t smell.*

I want so badly to come alive and tell them it is the smell of death. It is the smell of their imminent doom at the hands of a superpowerful crimefighter. But I can't blow my cover just yet. First they need to unbuckle the leather contraption and unstrap my wrists from the chair. Then I will come to life.

I can hear some muffled laughs. A few footsteps walk to a stop nearby, and then someone shrieks. It's all followed up by —sh-sh-sh-sh — sounds around me.

One of the white-coats asks, Is he alive?

Someone takes a pulse at my neck, while another white-coat undoes the wriststraps, and another takes off the headstrap. I can feel their hands all over me.

I think: if I want to escape, I have got to get my cape back and make a run for it. I have to escape now. This is my only chance. I can do this. I'm a superhero.

I open my eyes wide. All the white-coats look at me shocked. Their jaws drop. I punch the doctor-type nearest me, an upper cut to the head. He hits the ground hard. Another doctor-type tries to strap me back in, while another holds my arms back. I use my superpowerful strength to push them off of me. At the same time, I knee the white-coat with the straps in the gut and elbow the one from behind partly on the face and neck. Both go down for the count. More white-coats regroup to attack me.

I kick one doctor-type with both feet in the chest, hop over him, and land with a running start for the chamber door. A few doctor-types grab at me as I charge full speed ahead toward the door, where a white-coat is already positioned. I lower my shoulder and blast through the thick drab green-coated metal door. I completely level the frightened doctor-type but he lunges at me anyway. I skirt around him, grab my cape off the back of the chair, and scan quickly for an escape route.

I only see two options: go through several advancing white-coats, the front door and down the hall to the parking lot stairs or try jumping out the open window.

The whole scene comes to a halt when Mom walks into the room. Even the doctor-types freeze. They don't seem to know what to do.

A look of confusion washes over Mom's face, then horror at the sight of hospital staff scattered, injured on the floor, and several now trying to approach me. I can only imagine how bizarre all this must seem to her.

What in the world is going on here? Mom asks nobody in particular.

Joey? Her voice is angry and confused, Joey, what are you doing?

Sensing I wasn't paying attention, the white-coats try to make a move for me.

With my cape in hand, without thinking, I go to jump out the hospital window.

I miss it. Instead I crash into the brick wall like the Incredible Hulk, breaking through to the other side.

I hear Mom's scream; the white-coats all yell.

I fall through the air.

The window is on the first floor of the building so the fall is short. I land feet-first into a bunch of shrubbery. In front of me, I read a sign with gold lettering: St. Charles Hospital Audiology Clinic.

I hate this place.

Mom and the white-coats stick their heads out of the window. All their faces look shocked. I take off running again. I feel somewhat bad for trampling through the garden with its the orange, purple and yellow flowers in full bloom. I try to hop and skip over them as I run through a garden area. When I finally make it to the edge of the garden, there is a grassy knoll and I spot the woods far off. If I can make it to the woods, I can make it to freedom. I turn on my supersonic speed and rocket across the lawn toward the woods.

Behind me I can see white-coats climbing out the window. They give chase. Mom chases too. She waves her palm, screaming, Joey. I can see her red hair, bobbing up and down as she runs.

I'm too scared to turn back. So I keep running for the woods ahead. I'm almost out of breath with all the panic. I keep looking over my shoulder to see if anyone is gaining on me. When I see no one is close, I slow down some, then skip backwards. I can see those old people look very out of shape. They are all struggling to keep up. I could run for miles if I had to. They will never catch me.

A little ways into the woods, it occurs to me I have been holding my cape in my hands. I could have been wearing it this whole time. I could have been using its superpowers to fly. So I wrap the cape around my neck and take off running again. I imagine myself flying, stretching my arms out Superman-style.

I fly farther into the woods with the cape on my back. I don't see any white-coats following behind me anymore. They must have given up. I notice Mom stops following. She starts to go in the opposite direction, back over the grassy knoll. I can no longer see her. I wonder: where she is going?

I don't want to lose her. But I'm also not going back to Old Sparky. Then it comes to me. I think I know where Mom is going. She will be at Grammas'. I need to head west. Grammas' Sweet Shop and Ice Cream Parlor is right next to Billie's 1890 Saloon at the Main Street and East Main Street intersection, about a block south of the ferry docks. Mom will know to meet me there. Grammas' is always where we go after Old Sparky.

With my cape powering me, I fly farther and farther into the woods, heading westward to Grammas'. After what feels like a few miles, I come across a tree fort camouflaged with brush. I set down on the ground in front of the tree, take in the fort and the surrounding area. I notice there is no ladder on the tree trunk to get up into the fort.

This makes me curious. Who would build a fort without a ladder? How am I going to get up there?

No problem, I think. I'll just fly up there. I tighten my cape around my neck and with a running start try to take off into the air. I jump and gravity brings me right back down to the ground.

No problem, I think, I'll just try again.

With another running start, I take off again, only to fall face forward into a bush. I brush myself off and get back up. I start walking in circles underneath the fort, looking up into the tree to look for ways to get up there and for how the fort is made. I can see the fort is built with boat wood and rusted aluminum sheet metal. I'm impressed.

I think to myself: this fort builder knows his materials. Everybody knows boat wood is top-quality fort building material because it lasts in wet and harsh weather. The aluminum sheet metal makes for decent roofing too. When I look at the fort more carefully, I can make out a blue plastic bucket tied to white rope and a pulley system just outside the deck area flanking the door. That's clever, I think. I keep looking up into the tree fort but there doesn't seem to be anyone in there.

I yell, Hello?

I wait a minute or so for a response.

I try again, louder this time, Hello? Hello?

No answer.

I pick up a rock from the ground, about the size of a golf ball and aim for the fort's flooring above me. The rock bounces off the boat wood floorboards and rockets back to Earth. It's like the boat wood is a super protective force field.

Hello? Anyone there?

I pick up the same rock again. I aim and throw with all my strength for the floorboards one more time. The rock bounces off the fort's floors and falls fast back down to the ground.

Hello? Hello?

I walk over to pick the rock up again. But when I look down, I see the rock landed right next to a brown cardboard shoebox. I'm curious what is inside of it so I pick up the box. I look at it; shake it. The box feels a bit soggy. It must have been rained on. I open the lid, look inside the shoebox, and there are a pair of brown leather shoes. These are oddly square shaped shoes. But they look brand-new.

Why would someone just leave new shoes lying around in the woods? I wonder if these shoes belong to the person who made this fort?

The first thing I notice about the odd shoes are the really long spikes on them. Each spike is long enough, I guess, to be used as a tiny knife.

I say aloud, Yu culd kill someun wit' deez shoes.

I touch the tip of one spike with my finger. I'm startled when the tip pricks skin on my finger and it starts to bleed a bit. I pull the shoes out of the box and a piece of paper falls out. I pick up the paper and look at it. The paper is blank on both sides so I just crumble it up and toss it. I sit down on the ground with the shoes, place the shoebox to my side, take off my sneakers, and tie on the new shoes. I tie the knots and stand up to walk around and try the shoes out. They are about the right size, just a little bit smaller than my feet. The shoes feel snug. I run a few steps to see how the shoes feel. Each step I take is like a stab into the ground with the spikes. I almost have to yank my legs out of the ground after each step. It occurs to me then what these shoes are for.

I hop over to the base of the tree with the fort, jump up, grab onto a branch, and thrust my right shoe into the tree to start climbing. I climb the length of the tree up to the base of the fort, and then hop over the railing and onto a short deck area. The tree fort is huge. Its size reminds me of the cabanas on the beach down the road from my house.

I stand on the deck area and look down from where I just came. It's a long ways down, farther than it looked going up for some reason. I sit down and strip off the shoes so I can walk around without stabbing the floors.

I yell again, Hello? Anyone here?

No answer.

I walk over to the other side of the deck area, where there is a door.

I bang on it hard with my fist.

Hello? Hello? Anyone here?

No answer.

I look at the door. It has a latch on it but no lock. I undo the latch and the door swings wide open. I can't really see too good inside the fort, it's dark. My eyes adjust a bit and I walk into the fort structure.

I yell, Hello?

No answer.

It's so dark inside the fort, I have to walk with my hands out in front of me to feel what I'm walking into. I walk the length of the floor all the way to the far wall. When I look back I can see the light coming through the open door. It is then that I can make out the shapes in the room.

I see a table, some chairs, a bed, and a desk. I walk over to the desk and see that it has a white votive candle like the ones in church on it. Next to the candle is a blue BIC Lighter. I'm not allowed to play with matches or lighters but I know how to use them because I'm an altar boy and do the candle lighting sometimes for Saturday Mass. I light the candle with the BIC and see that the side of the candle illuminates an image of the cross. It kind of spooks me some. I place the lit candle down on the desk and look around the room.

I can see more clearly the table, chairs, and the desk are made of wood. The bed is made of metal. It has an orange wool blanket on it. I notice by the bed there is a black chest so I walk over to check it out, grabbing the candle so I can see more easily. At the foot of the bed, I sit and look at the chest. It's plain with silver metal hinges and a Master lock fastened on the front. I'm disappointed because I wanted to look and see what was inside. I yank on the lock a bit to see if it will come loose. The lock doesn't budge. I realize there is a nightstand against the wall. I place the candle on the nightstand so I can use both hands on the lock. I yank some more. No luck. The lock is tight. I just sit there on the edge of the bed on the orange blanket. I think: this is such a cool secret hideaway.

I look around the room for something else that might catch my interest. Nothing does. The room is very bare except for the furniture. I look back at the candle on the nightstand and notice there is a screwdriver on top of it. I grab the screwdriver and try to jam it into the lock to see if I can bust open the chest. It doesn't work. I get frustrated and toss the screwdriver onto the bed.

I really want to know what is inside that chest. What could it be?

I sit there on the bed for a few minutes. All of the sudden an idea comes to me. I take the screwdriver and sit myself cross-legged on the floor next to the chest. When I look at the back of the chest, I see two hinges on it, each with four screws. I laugh out loud.

Easy, I say aloud to no one.

With the screwdriver, I unscrew the chest hinges and pop open the chest. I'm so excited to see what is inside. I stand up, take the candle from the nightstand, and hold it over the chest. I can't believe my eyes: a green shield and white helmet sit inside all bright and shiny.

I blurt out loud, all excited: I found a secret superhero stash! Now I have something to go with my cape!

I take out the green shield. On the inside there is a cloth sleeve to place the arm into to hold the shield upright. I'm so thrilled by this find. I look at the front of the shield, it is green with a big white oval in the middle. I pull out the white helmet, it looks like a futuristic football helmet without the facemask. That too has an oval on each side but they are colored green like the shield. I carefully put the shield down on the bed and try on the helmet. It feels like a real superhero helmet. Now I have a real superhero outfit.

I wonder what the shield can be used for? What about the helmet? Do they have superpowers?

It comes to me: next time Mom takes me to the electric chair, I'll fight the white-coats off with the shield! They can't fry my brain with this helmet on!

Oh, no! Oh, no! I say, I forgot about Mom!

I grab both the shield and the helmet, blow out the candle, and run out the door. I throw the shield and helmet down to the ground and climb down the tree, only to realize halfway down that I forgot to put the spike shoes back on. There is no use, I figure, in climbing back up since I've already made it halfway. I keep heading downward. I get to the bottom of the tree and put on my sneakers quick. Before I take off to run to Grammas', I put on the helmet, tighten my cape around my neck, and put the shield under my arm. I run as fast as I can, thinking about poor Mom waiting and worrying about me at Grammas'.

When I finally make my way out of the woods it opens up into a housing development. I run through the street. It reminds me a lot of my own street where we live, even though the houses seem so much older and bigger. They look like the usual houses close to the water with their big barns to cover big boats parked in them. Some houses even have seashells for driveways. A few houses I pass walking along the road have canoes and kayaks lying on their lawns and rowboats and sailboats sitting in their driveways. It looks like such a fun place to live.

The shield is a bit heavy to carry so I have to stop every now and then to rest. I don't mind because I like to look at the houses. At one point, while resting for a few minutes, I notice the house in front of me has a very large boat with four fancy-looking motors on the back. It sits atop a trailer backed up to a blue Ford Bronco truck. I love that truck. Broncos are my favorite. I have every color Bronco Matchbox car made by Hotwheels.

I want so badly to check out the Bronco but I need to keep going to make it to Grammas'. I pick up the shield and walk-jog some more. I see a sign for South Street so I keep walking until I make out a familiar landmark, the red brick church we always pass on the way into the village of Port Jeff. Grammas' is just a little ways more down on Main Street. I'm so excited. I'm so very close.

When I get to the corner where the red brick church sits and Main Street, I stop and rest again with the shield. After a minute or so, I head north on the sidewalk toward the dockyards. After a few minutes, I can see the black glass of the storefront and the famous red neon sign in cursive letters.

It reads: Grammas' Sweet Shop and Ice Cream Parlor.

I'm almost there. I can almost taste my favorite ice cream – mint chocolate chip – on an old-fashioned waffle cone. Everything at Grammas' is homemade. When I finally get to the front of Grammas', I put down the shield and watch Mom's car pull up to the curb next to me. I'm surprised she didn't beat me here.

I thought for sure she would have been here before me. She had the car and I was walking so I don't know what took her so long. She jumps out of the car, walks straight over to me.

Mom asks, Have you lost your mind? Every one of those people at St. Charles were chasing after you. What were you thinking?

Before I can answer, she realizes I'm wearing the helmet and holding the shield. She asks, Joey, where did you get those from?

They're mine, I say.

No they're not, Joey. Where did you get them?

I cry. It is the only way to distract her. For sure, I think, Mom's going to punish me and make me return the helmet and shield. I cry really, really hard and make lots of loud noises. I can see Mom getting all uncomfortable because I'm making a scene in public.

Mom glosses over the helmet-shield conversation for now and says, Joey, those people at the hospital are trying to help you. I'm trying to get you a new hearing aid. You understand they need to test you. That testing booth is not a gas chamber.

I never said it was a gas chamber. It's an electric chair. I look at her and wonder if Mom ever listens.

Gas chamber. Electric chair. They're the same thing, Joey. Stop playing around. I can see she is losing her patience. But she doesn't.

Mom, a gas chamber is totally different than an electric chair. One kills you with gas, the other electricity. They are not the same thing. I argue and wait for her to realize that I'm right. She redirects me. That is always her trick to get out of these talks.

Mom asks me a question I'm not supposed to answer. Then she has a conversation with herself. I just stand there on the sidewalk and listen to her: Do you want to get some ice cream? Let's go to Grammas' since we're here…

She goes on, …I can use the pay phone to call the hospital and let them know we'll reschedule. Come on. And she goes on some more, What are these people going to think of me? They're going to think I'm a horrible mother. Until finally, Let's go before they turn this into a manhunt for a kid with a cape…and, well, I guess, a shield and football helmet.

Superhero helmet, I correct Mom.

She smiles, sees that I see she smiled, and laughs to herself. Mom picks up the shield and says, I'll carry this. Move it. Go, go get inside.

We go into Grammas' and I take it all in: the cool swivel stools with their shiny red cushions and gold sparkles; the rainbow of sweets like candy and ice cream in the glass case; the black and white checkered floors; and all those dusty mirrors and grainy pictures on the wall of the Port Jeff docks. Grammas' is always the same.

Mom places the shield up on top of a nearby stool and looks at me. She can see I'm all excited and says, Go ahead, jump on a stool and order whatever you want. She looks at the ice cream guy with the apron on, drying his hands on a towel, Where are the payphones?

He jokes, Are you both superheroes? Nice shield, Ma'am. The ice cream man winks at Mom and says, In the back by the ladies room, Ma'am.

He looks down at me, Nice cape and helmet, fella. He doesn't realize the shield is mine. What can I get you little fella?

Mom pulls me by my chin to her face to I can read her lips, I'll be right back. I've got to call the audiologist at St. Charles and let them know you are alright.

I say, K. Then look to the ice cream man and say, The shield is not my Mom's, it's mine. Mint chocolate chip on a waffle cone, please.

Oh, well, *excuse* me, he says.

When Mom gets back she has a coffee, black with no sugar. I lick my ice cream slowly. Every now and then, Mom takes a napkin, licks it, and wipes my face. I hate that so I block her with my elbow. She gives me the Look, says, You're being ridiculous.

Mom?

Yes.

Why am I hard of hearin'?

Because you had double pneumonia when you were six weeks old.

What is dubble mona?

Pneumonia. It's like a really bad chest cold.

Oh. That why you make me take dat yucky syrup when I'm sick?

Yes.

Do yu take dat yucky syrup too?

No, there is yucky syrup for adults.

Is it yuckier than mine?

Yes. Way yuckier.

When I grow up, can I take kid syrup instead of big people syrup?

I don't know. We'll have to ask the doctor about that. You ready to go?

Mom picks up the shield and pays the guy at the cash register. He gives me a free lollipop and says, Hey, hey you, with the cape and helmet. Again, he doesn't say anything about the shield. What superhero are you?

I look at him, say, Depends.

I can see Mom shoot him the Look, like he doesn't understand he just opened a can of worms. Mom wants to go. But I want to talk with the ice cream man.

Mom tries to take my hand but I won't let her. I tell him, It depends. Sometimes I'm Superman so I can fly. Sometimes I'm Batman so I can drive the Batmobile. Or Spiderman so I can climb walls. Or Captain America, Wonder Woman, or Robin. Or the Hulk when I have a temper too. Right Mom?

She laughs, Oh you sure can be a Hulk sometimes, yanking on me, Come on, let's go, say thank you for the lollipop and good-bye to the man.

Thank you, Bye!

SEVEN

"Be good, Joey"

It is the spring of 1980, I'm four years old. I feel so excited to see the small yellow school bus pull up to the curb outside our ranch-style home. This is my first day of preschool. My mother tells me, "Be good, Joey," and walks me to the open bus door where a woman sits behind the wheel, grinning at me.

The bus driver lady talks to me, "Hi, Joey," and looks at my mother.

I look up to her, "Hi."

"Come on, you can hop those steps. Show the bus driver lady," my mother gives me a little push forward.

"Okay, Mommy." I hop the two steps up.

At the top of the steps, I turn around, "Bye, Mommy," and wave.

My mother waves back to me. The bus driver gets up from behind the wheel, walks with me down the aisle, takes to me my seat, and buckles me in with a seatbelt. She walks back to the front of the bus, waves to my mother, closes the door, and we drive off.

I sit there in the seat alone. No one else is on the bus except me. When we make our first stop, I unbuckle my seatbelt by myself and get up to go to school.

The bus driver lady looks at me, "Joey, we're not at school yet. We have to pick up some other kids, okay?"

"Okay," I tell her but I don't understand.

I stand there at the front of the bus.

"Joey, you need to sit down. Joshua and his mommy are coming to get on the bus with us, okay?"

"Okay." I walk back to my seat and put on the seatbelt.

A few minutes later I can hear the bus driver lady say something to someone. There are other voices too. An older kid comes down the aisle and sits across from me. He puts on his seatbelt. The older kid does not say anything or look at me. He waves out the window when we drive away.

We keep stopping again and again to pick up more kids. The ride to the preschool is long and I fall asleep in my seat watching the traffic on the road, already exhausted by the excitement of my new day. When the bus finally arrives at the school, I lift myself up from the seat to peek out the window. All I can see is a plain white cement-walled building. It reminds me of the hospital my mother takes me to for ear tests.

A woman leads us off the bus through the doors of the preschool into our classroom. Some of my classmates are in wheel-chairs; some walk with sticks in their hands; others, it seems, have nothing visibly special about them. The school is buzzing with gossipy mouths, and the adults in the classroom explain to the returning students that the school was broken into over the holidays and many of their toys are missing. I wonder how someone could break into the school with so many bars on the windows.

They then take us down the hallway to a gymnasium, where immediately I spot an above-ground pool. Strange, I think to myself: there isn't any water in it. The pool is filled with blue, green, red and yellow plastic balls. I climb the short ladder and jump in. This, I decide, is where I am going to spend my day. A woman grabs me from the side of the pool, lifting me to the ground; she takes off my Buster Brown shoes and lifts me back into the pool.

After some time, the adults tell us we have to come out of the ball pool, pointing to the now open door to the playground. It is a drab day with the sun only peeking through the clouds occasionally. The same woman lifts me out of the pool, puts my shoes on and directs me outside by leading my shoulders, walking behind me. I'm not sure what to do until I see the monkey bars. I'm a big climber, so I take off fast and mount the structure swiftly. I look around at the different children playing nearby and the other equipment, but nothing competes with the monkey bars for my attention. A little boy with a bowl-cut like mine climbs the monkey bars. The two of us are the only children on the playground without a wheelchair or sticks. We both sit on top of the jungle gym and look each other over curiously.

I say, "Hi."

He says nothing.

I repeat, "Hi."

He motions for me to follow him down the monkey bars. I tag along, climbing headfirst toward the ground Spiderman-style. We end up behind a row of slides, near the ladders and he taps my shoulder to look at him.

My new friend shows me his hands. They soar and dive like airplanes in the sky. I watch in wonderment. What is he doing?

"Is this a game?" I ask.

The boy just motions some more. Then he grabs my hands and makes them move through space. I'm unsure but it seems like fun. Next he separates himself from me, shows me how to make my hands move like his. I watch his right middle and pointy fingers come together and tap the four outstretched fingers of his left hand. After, he uses the same fingers to tap the underside of his outspread fingers, and then slides the middle and pointy fingers between them. In brusque motions, he slaps his hands together and slides the right hand off the left palm away from his body.

He shows me the hand moves a few more times. When he finally starts to look at me with excitement, I think I'm getting it. Suddenly, the woman who took off and put on my shoes comes rushing over. She slaps both our hands and makes an angry face. I'm confused and scared because I'm not allowed to get in trouble.

EIGHT

The Road from Schoolchild to Subaltern Subject

Storytelling is my way of agitating, inviting the reader into a personal narrative to confront the existential in research on young deaf children and schooling. Deaf children face overwhelming inequity living in an adult and hearing-centered world. Due to language modality differences and/or preferences, deaf children's thoughts and feelings are often ignored or subsumed by the more message-savvy educational and medical/rehabilitative community. These messages saturate the current cultural climate that emphasizes the physical construction of deafness, ignoring the Deaf culture perspective. Even more, young deaf children are interpellated by our audist society and their marginalized position becomes internalized. Over the course of life for d/Deaf children, this internalized oppression is sometimes entirely accepted, sometimes resisted, and sometimes transformed. Memories are organic, and our life histories are a continually evolving process; as past experiences are (re)created they inform and are informed by the present.

Like many who have been/are marginalized, I hold a deep suspicion of grand theories and narratives (Said, 1978; Spivak, 1988; Loomba, 1998; Kaomea, 2005). For the marginalized, subaltern scholar, essentializing and generalizing ways of thinking are clues that something is awry (Lincoln and Guba, 1985; Said, 1993; Zizek, 1992). I am most interested in the contradictions, tensions, and moments where epistemic violence surfaces. I use the term epistemic violence to challenge our phonocentric society to (re)conceptualize physical versus cultural constructions of deafness, where the former serves to silence and the latter to empower the lives of young children.

To add depth and perspective to my autobiographical account of my journey from being deaf to Deaf, I interviewed my mother, sister, brother, doctoral advisor, and classmates, who are also friends, about their thoughts on my life. As I conducted and analyzed these interviews, I became aware of themes and tropes that weave across their utterances, providing me with a new understanding of my autobiography. Prior to interviewing my informants, I had written vignettes of salient memories from key moments in my life. In most cases my informants didn't remember these events and told me other stories about me. In the sections that follow I track back and forth between my various memories and the perspectives on my life of my informants.

In this book, I follow Tobin's (1997, 2000) and Kaomea's (2005) suggestion to view theory not as something we believe in but instead as a set of tools. For me, the idea of theory as a tool not only connects to my own family's roots as blue-collar, working-class (as they self-identify themselves) but also makes theory, which is often abstract, seem accessible. The idea of theory as a tool seems like something I can grab onto and a hold of, even as it remains literally intangible. I can imagine myself struggling with and muddling (Eisenhart, 2001) and losing patience with these theoretical tools. But even more important, the use of theory as a tool is a continual and, I argue, a critical (self-reflexive) reminder of how the way we see the world is influenced by which tool(s) we choose to use to examine it. Simply, thinking of theory as a tool is a testament to where I come from and where I want to go.

I use my life story as a research tool (Rolfe & MacNaughton, 2001). I also use my life story as a tool to inform my research viewpoint. This standpoint is the way I see, live, and think about the world in the past, present, and future. To paraphrase Edward Said's (1993) words of wisdom about the importance of ideological self-awareness: cultures are a theatre in which ideologies collide and we must be cognizant that ideologies inform one's theoretical stance(s). I recognize and avow my ideological stance to be epistemologically Deaf, meaning in this sense, that I value a Deaf cultural perspective as opposed to a physical construction of deafness, even though this was not the case as I was growing up. I saw myself as the "deaf kid" in my school and community, and these memories now inform much of what I think and do as an emerging scholar and storyteller. So it is in this way I use theory and my life story as a tool for research. The scholar informs the storyteller; the storyteller informs the scholar.

This chapter is a story about violence. It aims to travel the brutal road from schoolchild to subaltern subject through my memories of being a "deaf kid" in preschool. The violence begins early, as children with deafness like me are forced to navigate the binary battlefield of able/disabled, deaf/hearing, and normal/abnormal, within a system where the medical, educational, and business communities reign and "[g]enerally speaking, all the authorities exercising individual control function according to a double mode; that of binary division and branding" (Foucault, 1995, p. 199). The vignette about my first day of preschool vividly exhibits the workings of these binary, marginalizing forces in my life and the ensuing epistemic violence (both literally, due to the hand slap and figuratively through the impression this memory has on me today).

The vignette raises various questions: Was it against school rules to sign? What were the epistemic views at the time on deafness and signing? Why did the adult slap the hands of two children signing? Was my new friend teaching me bad words? Were they words?

The idea that someone can be punished for learning a language is not new. Being punished for literacy, for reading and writing and signing is not new news. There is a long history of learning going underground in marginalized communities and rights to literacy being contested (for example, Cornelius, 1983; Skutnabb-Kangas & Phillipson, 1994; Phillipson, 2000; Del Valle, 2003; McCarty, 2005; Skutnabb-Kangas, 2007; Gundaker, 1998, 2007). For many historically marginalized communities across the ages, "the promise of literacy was as great as the punishment for acquiring it" (McDermott and Raley, 2007, p. 1826). That day in preschool was the first time I had ever been punished for language (though, much later I struggled through adolescence and on with a taste for salty language, much to my mother's chagrin). I learned on that day that literacy could lead to punishment. I also learned literacy could be a powerful tool.

Many minority culture members have struggled to gain access to and have been punished for a language and literacy that an oppressive majority society wanted to control. But often the lure of literacy is too much to resist. In some cases, literacy has literally conferred freedom. There are reports of African-American slaves who learned to write and then wrote their own passes to go north to freedom. If caught by disapproving slave owners, offending slaves paid a heavy price to learn to read and write. With amputations, whippings, and beatings, "[f]ew such demonstrations were necessary to effectively stifle the desire to read among most slaves, and to establish a mythology about the dangers of reading and writing" (Cornelius, p. 174). Popular myths that there were widespread laws against slaves learning to read and write were in actuality wrong, there were in fact only four Southern states that passed laws against teaching slaves (Cornelius, 1983). The power of literacy is coveted by both the marginalizers and marginalized.

When I was a preschooler back in the late 1970s there were no laws against teaching sign language in schools. But the memory illustrates the dangers of literacy — the wrong kind of literacy, that is, was still very much alive at that time. Referencing ethnographic work on literacy by Brian Street (1985) and Elsie Rockwell (2005), McDermot and Raley (2007) point out that "some people having literacy is really bad for people who do not read and write in prescribed ways" (p. 1826). For African-American slaves the mythology about reading and writing based on the belief that it was dangerous was fueled by the white oppressor desire to continue slavery and suppress liberation. The tactic was to punish. To parallel this with my experience getting my hand slapped as a preschooler, the stuff that makes up the mythology may have changed but not the tactic. The mythology about *signing* based on the belief that it was dangerous and that is was not the prescribed literacy was fueled by the hearing oppressor desire to fix the Deaf and suppress manual language (and force speech). The tactic, once again, was to punish.

I can't go back and interview the teacher who slapped our hands to seek out her justification for her action. I can speculate that she thought her punitive actions were in our best interests and that the school's approach to working with deaf children reflected scientific understanding of the times. Danforth, Taff, and Ferguson (2006) assert that "scientific ways of viewing social issues and possible solutions" assume "that the problems of poverty and social deviance could be solved by professionals whose...expertise was based in science" (p. 14). But rather than attempt to tell the story of my life from the perspective of those who wielded power over me, I choose to offer counter-stories. Counter-storytelling scholars endeavor to provide counter-discourses in order to validate and value lived experiences (e.g., Ladd, 2003, 2005; Mutua and Swadener, 2004; Ladson-Billings and Tate, 2006; Delgado and Stefanic, 2001; Solarzano and Yasso, 2002) that are critically needed to respond to prevailing discourses that unquestionably valorize majoritarian perspectives, as "culture, the great enabler of humanity, is also and in the same movement the great disabler"

(Varenne and McDermott, 1999, p. 142). Counter-story telling is a strategy for challenging this disabling.

In trying to determine how the experience of my first day at preschool enabled/disabled my life history, I asked my mother for her reflections on that day. She told me, "If that happened, Joey, I doubt the teacher meant to stop you from [learning] sign language; you were probably not supposed to be hiding behind those swings, or she [the teacher] just didn't know any better."

My mother on numerous occasions shared with me her feelings of being a failing parent, and for her the tension of this conversation leads her to take a defensive tone. She knows this discussion will inevitably bring up the topic of me not learning sign language; we have had this talk before.

"The teacher was trying to control me, Mom." I respond.

She counters, "Joey, you are fortunate that you speak so well. Many people don't even know you're hard of hearing when you talk. When you were in preschool, the teachers, everybody was worried about you. No one except me could understand you. So, maybe, she was trying to stop you from learning sign language to help. It wasn't right of her, but maybe she thought she was helping."

In a society that unquestionably values hearing, I was beginning to become conscious of power at a very young age. Varenne and McDermott (1999) view "the school as historically constructed, always already there" and the fact that I remember this incident so many years later, thinking of it often, even periodically replaying the hand movements, I wonder how my rendering of the story reflects a retroactive re-presentation and reinterpretation of the event (p. 155).

With Foucault in mind, we can see in the slapping of children's hands by a teacher under the sway of audism the workings of the humanizing process of normalizing and disciplining the failing, unruly body. The imprint of this experience is a part of my body memory. "Moral claims of humanism" justify the hand slap, as the teacher, operating within the discursive understandings of the time, saw fit to intervene physically in order to condition us to a phonocentric expectation – to use voice only, and not hands, to talk (Foucault, 1995, p. 30). For this teacher, the line between hearing and deaf was static and fixed. Varenne and McDermott (1999) emphasize the importance of using cultural, historical analyses to uncover deficit-laden preconceptions. The reasoning behind the teacher's (and, by extension, the school's) "humanizing" physical intervention is that it is representative of the society's (re)production of cultural (and physical) perspectives (Nasir and Hand, 2006). My experiences at the preschool are an example of the localization of national (or international) contexts where the cultural climate gives credence only to cultural-deficit and physical-deficit constructions of deafness, as well as the valuing of speech over sign language.

From that moment on in my child-eyed outlook, I always viewed signing (I would not know the term American Sign Language until much later) as a secretive and potentially dangerous medium of expression. I do not know how much my own experience is like or unlike other deaf children, but I imagine I was neither the first nor the last child to be restrained physically from learning a manual/visual language. Said (1993) observes of constructions of the Orient that "the horrifically predictable disclaimer that 'we' are exceptional" keeps alive "notions about bringing civilization to primitive or barbaric peoples"; the same could be said about the general rehabilitative goals of deaf and special education (pp. xi-xxiii).

As a four-year old wanting to please adults and steer clear of trouble I felt the power of the teacher's gaze and of the sting of her hand slap, feeling, and internalizing in her response the expectations of normalization. In my worldview, the panoptic gaze of adults was now associated with the use of signs, a lesson my new friend seems to have already learned in light of his attempt to conceal what we were doing together. It was the first time I realized I might need to use the tactic of concealment to get by in this world. I learned to conceal my feelings, thoughts, (mis)understandings, and what I heard or did not hear in order to seem like everyone else and not get literally or figuratively slapped. I learned to intuit based on body language, facial expressions, and context. This is still one of my tactics of meaning making, even today, sometimes employed successfully and other times not.

My mother spoke about how skillful I was as a young child, intuiting what was happening, "It always seems to everyone that you understand what is going on. I watch you. I know you don't understand sometimes. Even when you were little, I'd tell everyone: 'Make sure he [Joey] is facing you'; everyone thought it was so you could read their lips; I knew you needed to see the whole face to understand." Joe Tobin commented on my intuitive tactics as a graduate student: "I saw you struggle with some things...little things, I became aware that you sometimes missed things in class. I see times when things must be hard. You always did an extraordinarily good job of understanding what was going on, but I could see you sometimes intuit wrongly."

As a child and today, I internalize(d) what I intuit(ed) – that I was/am deaf and dumb. I was always already deaf and dumb. The look on people's faces throughout my years in school: exasperation for repeating themselves, disbelief at the stupidity of my responses, even outright contempt for what they saw as my "choosing not to listen." I bought into the idea that I was insensitive and that I didn't try hard enough to 'listen' because so many told me it was the case that it had to be true. In this way, Althusser's conception of interpellation provides an apt description of how this always already disabled-ness and voiceless-ness seeped into the core of who I am today.

"You're hard on others, Joey, because they were so hard on you," my younger sister, Jill tells me, "You learned how to use words to hurt people because they did it to you all the time."

"Who was so hard on me?" I ask.

"Teachers and kids at school. They saw you wearing hearing aids and thought you were deaf and dumb. They sure were wrong, Dr. Joe." Jill laughs.

Jill goes quiet and starts to say something and stops.

"What were you going to say," I ask.

"I was thinking about all the times you try to talk with me about being proud of my Korean heritage and being adopted," Jill goes on. "You trying to teach me Korean, taking me to Korean restaurants, telling me weird facts about Korea, telling me to visit there" she pauses.

"And…" I say rather impatiently.

"You do the same thing with being Deaf," she says, "You're proud now."

Jill is right. Now, I laugh when I read Brenda Jo Brueggemann's (1999) reflection on having watched the same movies as others, but in her visually cued, non-hearing world seeing an entirely different film. I watched for horror in the lines of actor's faces and for sadness to set in the lips. I cherish the way I see the world now. There are many autobiographical accounts written by d/Deaf informants detailing life events growing up with deafness (e.g., notably Bertling, 1994; Wright, 1994; Brueggemann, 1999; Thoryk, Roberts, and Battistone, 2001; Padden and Humphries, 2005; Mitchell, 2006). More recently Paddy Ladd (2003) has come up with the term Deafhood to describe the practice of dialoging about the lives of people with deafness by d/Deaf people themselves. Ladd (2003) notes:

> Deafhood is not…a 'static' medical condition like 'deafness'. Instead, it represents a process – the struggle by each Deaf child, Deaf family and Deaf adult to explain to themselves and each other their own existence in the world. In sharing their lives with each other as a community, and enacting those explanations rather than writing books about them, Deaf people are engaged in a daily praxis, a continuing internal and external dialogue (p. 3).

Today there exist counter-stories about living life with deafness, most notably in print and other mediums; however, since d/Deaf community members may feel ambivalence about the writing medium, perhaps, not the preferred choice of narrative considering the visual nature of sign or lack of dexterity with written language, enough of these stories are not accessible to the larger phonocentric society to counteract scientivism's dominance of public discourses (e.g., Brueggemann, 1999, 2004; Ladd, 2003; Breivik, 2005). I now think the road from schoolchild to subaltern was foreshadowed by this first day in preschool, the experience of internalizing the normalizing expectations of schooling would replicate itself over and over again.

NINE

"R2-D2, R2-D2, R2-D2"

It is the fall of 1980, Ronald Reagan gains momentum in the race for president in Cold War America, Izod is in and bell bottoms out, as *Star Wars: The Empire Strikes Back* takes over the imaginations of children across the country. I'm four going on five, playing on the Sylvan Avenue elementary school playground during recess, running from the swings to the riding horse with a large spring bolted into the ground. With heckling children below, I sit proudly atop the metal mare swatting away hands prying at my ears. Classmates obsessed with the peach-colored gadgetry, wires, plastic tubes and buttons in my ears, finally knock my bilateral hearing aids to the ground, chanting, "R2-D2, R2-D2, R2-D2."

Without thinking, my hands-turned-fists flail about, striking several children on their heads. Quickly Mrs. Tarry, our kindergarten teacher, pulls me away and sets me down on the bench with sad eyes. I'm full of tearful anger and rage that can't be consoled. She turns to the mean kids and yells something at them. I don't hear her words.

Mrs. Tarry says something to me.

I can't hear her. Her lips move.

"What?" I ask. I'm having a hard time catching my breath because I'm crying so hard. I look at her face and pay attention really hard.

Mrs. Tarry says something again.

I don't hear her. Mrs. Tarry's face lights up. She puts her hands over my ears. Her lips read, "Oh, my God."

She realizes I've lost my hearing aids and starts crawling all over the playground to look for them. I sit on the bench and watch and cry. I can see the mean kids standing on the side of the playground. They point at Mrs. Tarry, me, then back to Mrs. Tarry and me and talk to each other.

Mrs. Tarry gathers my aids and tries to put them back in my ears. I take them from her and put them in my ears. One is broken. When I stand up from the bench, she tenderly takes my hand and walks me through the classroom, down the kindergarten wing to the main office. I'm scared stiff, knowing they will call my mom. I sit on a chair and can see Mrs. Tarry speaking with the secretary. Mrs. Tarry gently taps my head on the way out, mouthing something. I'm confused by her reassuring look. The secretary leads me into principal's office, a wood-paneled chamber with the musty aroma of old-school authority, and points to a chair facing a large desk. Fixed to my leather seat, I notice her sad eyes too. A grandfatherly man walks in, exchanges a few words with the secretary and sits down opposite me. He says, "Hi, Joey, I'm Mr. Weik."

I respond, "I'm sorry, Mr. White," thinking of my impending doom; I cry.

His eyes reveal a smile and his lips move, "My name is Mr. Weik," emphasizing the "K-uh" sound. He wears an attentive face for an adult, I think to myself.

He asks, "What happened, Joey?"

"I hit them," I say, looking over my shoulder, turning my body sideways, and pointing through the doorway, down the hall to where I guessed my classmates were.

As I turn around, he asks, "Why?"

"They called me a robot."

TEN

Robots, Superheroes, and Talking Identity

Children, much like adults, inhabit multiple identities that are not always clearly defined or necessarily lasting. When research on the marginalization of children with deafness describes children as pawns within an institutional system, there is a reification of the *deafing* (disempowering) and *dumbing* (silencing) of children with deafness. The complexity of making sense of identity work and of familiarizing (and defamiliarizing) identity talk requires attention to social interactions across multiple contexts. With some theoretical license, I borrow Stanton Wortham's (2006) idea that views identities as hybrid and circulating. My analysis focuses on the "meshing of local cognitive and metapragmatic models," where "power/knowledge or self/knowledge...develops at a shorter timescale than the one described by Foucault" (Wortham, 2006, p. 90). To do this, I will try to explicate the identity work that has informed my recollecting and telling of memories of my life in deafness and in my reactions to the interviews about my life I conducted with others. Identities, much like memories, are organic and shape-shifting, always dependent on context. Life histories tell us more about how we use memories in our identity work than about the memories themselves.

I intend to use these ideas to tease out identity/self constructions based on the interplay between my memories and my informants' comments, as related to the themes of robots and superheroes that emerged in my reflections and then construction of this narrative. There is a doubling and collapsing of time and context at work here as I create my narrative by negotiating back and forth between my narrative account of my memories and the way I talk about and co-construct these memories with my informants (Kaomea, 2003, 2004). The memories in this account both of my long-ago and recent past are, therefore, simultaneously about who I was, who I became, and who I am now, as my identity is experienced, performed, and formed in my interactions with others.

In a recent conversation I shared with my mother the snapshot memory of being called a robot by those children on the playground over 25 years ago and she responds, "Joey, Mrs. Tarry and Mr. Weik were good people, they took such good care of you...loved you. Do you remember Mr. Weik, me, and you had to go looking for the hearing aids in the leaves? Mr. Weik was the one who found them. Always thought you threw them away...$1,000 for a hearing aid! How many hearing aids did you lose in school? My, they were $1,000 each. Mr. Weik was out there in his nice suit, looking through wet leaves to find pieces [of the hearing aids]. You wore bilateral aids from St. Charles. You told all the kids you were a superhero that had to wear them...we [the adults] used to laugh because we'd hear the kids talking about your superhero powers. You did what you had to do...to make it. So you did have superhero powers."

"I had superpowers?" I'm not sure where this is leading.

"Yes," she says, "They thought you were a superhero with superpowers because you wore hearing aids. They thought the hearing aids gave you superpowers."

"Why did they call me a robot?" I ask out loud, a question not only addressed to my mother.

"Maybe you're choosing to remember it that way, Joey." My mother reminds me of an oft-repeated saying of hers, "It is not what people say that people remember, but how they feel."

My mother and I both go quiet for a minute or so.

She blinks first, "So how did it make you feel?"

"Fucking pissed," I say quickly before remembering to temper my language.

"What made you angry, the name calling?" She sounds real sad.

"Not as much as them pushing and shoving me. I hated their touch." I think to myself about all those hands on me – the kids bullying, the adults poking and prodding me at St. Charles. My body memory remembers the alienation, stigma, and internalized sense of failure accompanying the normalizing of my body through teasing, bullying, and being overpowered physically and emotionally by professionals. Alessandro Duranti (1997) reminds us, "We often forget that the human body is the first instrument we experience...Our mouth, hands, eyes, feet and other body parts are the first mediating elements in our interaction with people" (p. 322). Duranti (1997) discusses how the spatio-temporal coordinates of interactions are shaped by the past, space, place, and meaning. Each provides a "microhistory of human interaction" that connects to the larger context of society (p. 322).

H-Dirksen Bauman (2004) merges Derrida's framing of our society as unquestionably, epistemically phonocentric with Foucault's idea of institutions serving as conduits of normality and deviance (in this case, of audism and deafness). Bauman offers an explanation of how Derridean phonocentrism meets Foucauldian institutionalization in our communities and schools, "Educational practices such as oralism...and mainstreaming are the institutionalization of our phonocentric and audist metaphysical orientation; the practices of these institutions then beget individual audist attitudes through daily practices, rituals, and disciplining Deaf bodies into becoming closer to normal hearing bodies" (Bauman, 2004, p. 245). I begin to wonder if it was really that I hated touch, which in retrospect I doubt was the case, or would it be more accurate to say it was the "disciplining touch" (both physically and verbally) that I hated?

This back and forth between my mother and me reflects something of our and the world's views of deafness both now and back then. Since I can't go back in time to ask my classmates about why they called me a robot, we can never really know. However, in examining the conversation with my mother involving the playground bullying, I can get at the root where my (re)collections and body memory converge with the phonocentric cultural climates of the past and present. How did/does my mother construct the meaning of robot and superhero? How did/do I?

I ask my mother, "Why do you think I remember they called me a robot that day and not a superhero?"

"They wanted to be mean, maybe, who knows why kids are mean, Joey. What makes you think robot is bad?"

"Well, it certainly didn't feel good, Mom. They were hitting me too."

"I remember them thinking you were a superhero with special powers. You remember them calling you a robot. They're just words – they're just words, remember."

"I know," I say unconvinced. I hesitate to push this too far. My mother is not just my informant in this self-investigation, helping make sense of my past and present— this is her story, too, the sufferings and the successes hers as well as mine. I want to tell her someday that I'm sorry for having always held her responsible for the pain I felt growing up in a phonocentric world. My mom, like me, interpellated audism; she as an always already failing parent, me as an always already failing child (Althusser, 1972; Kaomea, 2004).

In talking about memory work, Cheryl Mattingly and Linda Garro (2000) "highlight the role of narrative in communicating the remembered past. Narrative accounts convey the effort to make sense of the past from the perspective of the present," since past-remembering gives meaning to our daily life and constructed worlds (p. 71). In this sense, I use memory narratives not to make claims of accuracy about whether the children called me a robot or superhero but to contextualize the affective and cultural frameworks of the past (think back to my mother's advice about talk, where feelings are remembered over words).

As a scholar and storyteller, I aim to *show* how "d/Deaf and d/Dumb" *feels* (which I will examine in greater detail later). I aim to tease out the cultural work, both past and current, that goes into my identity (re)formation and self concept as they continuously alternate between the always already colonized self (deaf and dumb) and subaltern radical agitator (Deaf and Dumb). My daily world is constructed by the binaries of "d/Deaf and d/Dumb." These terms are always present in my struggles to reconcile my life history to my present self. As an adult, in telling my mother about my past childhood pain, I'm working through feelings of alienation, stigma, and internalized failure that are still part of my everyday world. Simultaneously, I'm connecting to feelings of acceptance, pride, and possibility by sharing with her and co-constructing a collective family memory. Cultural and self-knowledge serve as vehicles for interpreting meaning of past memories. Mattingly and Garro (2000), citing D'Andrade (1995), point out that "understandings about illness and treatment, like other aspects of cultural knowledge, are socially distributed within a cultural setting" (p. 73). Frederick Erickson (2004) discusses the situated nature of the cultural work that goes into talk. Erickson advises researchers to closely examine "the local conduct of talk...connecting it to the workings of the wider society" (p. 133).

For young children self-concept and identity are closely linked through personal, ecological, interpersonal, and internalized views of the conceptual self, "function[ing] as creator of meaning" (Torstenson-Ed, 2007, p. 64). Life histories mold self-concepts and identity, as the "telling" makes sense of past experience (Mattingly and Garro, 2000; Ochs and Capps, 2001). The writing down of these memories seems to give me a sense that they are somehow more legitimate, the telling of the robot story is both therapeutic and self-actualizing. If the cornerstone of narratives is storytelling and the accompanying meaning-making (Bruner, 1990; Mattingly and Garro, 2000; Ochs and Capps, 2001); then this leads us to the question: What meaning-making is happening in the memory discussions with my mother?

I want to further explore my family's collective memory. This time I turn to my brother to add another viewpoint to my robot memory and as well as to my recent talk with my mom. John is a little more than a year older than me. As siblings close in age, we spent much of our early lives together formulating our life histories in the countless hours we shared at the dinner table, car rides, and hanging around the kitchen. My older brother is the one who taught me the techniques and joys of co-storytelling; he is the best storyteller I know. I share with him the robot vignette and my notes from my conversation with our mom, simply asking, "What do you think?"

John, known for being cool and controlled, surprises me with the rawness of his response. I never before knew he thought this way. He starts off with a sarcastic laugh, "You should sue the schools...they were not prepared to handle you – they would say, 'Oh, my God, he's not normal, send him down the BOCES hallway'...everyone was scared to go down the BOCES hallway, that's where they kept the retards. What a shame...25 years ago, kids like you, down the BOCES hallway, it was horrible, they'd be like 'sshh...don't tell anybody in school, we have these kids, they look or talk funny, just put them in BOCES'...look what they did to kids like you, and those ELL [English Language Learners] kids then, uh, oh, he talks funny...did they know it was called Spanish? Same as you, deaf kid, why not have you go to a deaf school, learn ASL? Except for you, what are those other kids doing now? Did they graduate? Or did they find a new place to hide 'em?"

John, without the benefit of having read Foucault, hits on Foucauldian constructs of the panopticon, power/knowledge, and discursive practices. Foucault aptly notes: "The body serves as an instrument or intermediary" with "a whole army of technicians took over from the executioner, the immediate anatomist of pain: warders, doctors, chaplains, psychiatrists, psychologists, educationalists" leading to "an economy of suspended rights" (1995, p. 11). I can also clearly see the link between what John is saying and Foucauldian conceptions of power/knowledge happening on a shorter timescale, as discussed by Wortham (2006). And yet as he speaks I also feel myself wanting to distance myself from my brother's use of the term "retard." As an educator seeking social justice, I know the lineage of the term, and how it has been used to essentialize and mistreat people with a variety of disabilities.

I say to John, "Why do you use the word 'retards'?"

He pushes me, "Do you remember getting the world's smartest retard award in high school? How did that make you feel?"

"Embarrassed and proud, I guess," I say. I now remember using the term "world's smartest retard" as an adolescent. I remember accepting the county executive achievement award, learning at my arrival that it was awarded (but of course not with that title) each year to students with disabilities who demonstrated extraordinary (by normative standards) achievements in school. My mother and brother, I remember now, were offended for me, as students with various marked and unmarked disabilities were paraded in front of a crowd of politicians, educators, and families, citing our disabilities and accomplishments publicly, culminating in a group photo with a county executive for the newspapers. I resisted this identity as a disabled student who was doing better than might be expected, associating this label with my internalized feelings of alienation, stigma, and failure. I am, after all, the child of a mother who told me as a child and continues to say now that I did not then and do not now have a disability. My brother's comment triggers the memory in me of how conflicted I felt that night of the awards and about my growing realization that the identity I (co)constructed with my family did not fit with the larger world's vision of who I was.

Hugh Mehan (1993) introduces epistemological and ontogenetic questions about representations, by linking talk with institutional policies. His analyses push towards questioning power/knowledge and self/knowledge (re)formation(s). Writing about these memories from kindergarten (re)awakens feelings inside of me of sadness, happiness, and anger. Looking back I re-experience and feel the kindness of Ms. Tarry and Mr. Weik, the cruelty of the children's taunts, and bittersweet ambivalence of my high school award. As these feelings well up, I immediately calm myself, and I switch on my identity, a step removed as the autobiographer and ethnographer of my life whose task it is to analyze the tensions presented in this vignette. The construction of reality that I made (or that was made for me) as a young child about the world surrounding me was of a bleak, uncertain, and scary place. Like many children who have been marginalized, these memories are embedded in my body and mind and continue to inform who I am today. For example, as a scholar in the field of education, I am deeply sensitive to the impositions of schooling. Reading and writing have always been my escape, my therapy. To this list of coping strategies I recently have added conducting research.

In order to survive, I learned a form of self-management and self-improvement reminiscent of Foucault's "care of the self" – a never-ending determination to shape the person I wanted to be and still plan to be. It is a form of self-improvement that sees no end. The costs can be high, especially when the "improvement" seems to require that I "normalize" my mind and body. I spent my life trying to be hearing/non-deaf, and regardless of whoever's construction of hearing was the model, part of me has always known and felt that success in this self-improvement plan would mean giving myself a life sentence to a phonocentric prison. I just never knew how to articulate these feelings. My epistemology was under an audist regime; I was too busy trying to be the best hearing person I could be to consciously confront this dilemma and its implications.

My mother might be able to shed some light. "You know, the only thing I'd change, if you ask me? The only thing I would change, if I could change anything," my mother is trying to get at something; I know this because she always prefaces such talk with a rhetorical question. "I wish you'd reevaluate the overachieving. You put too much stress on yourself. You're afraid to fail. You internalize that fear."

"Why do you think I'm this way?"

"Because I'm that way, because I always told you that you had to work twice as hard. You did…then at some point you passed everyone…but kept working yourself too hard. You always wanted to be the teacher, wanted to know everything. It wasn't always fun, you kept going on fear. Some of your teachers didn't know what to do with you."

This all started to change once I learned about audism in graduate school and learned to apply post-colonial ideas to my own experiences. Part of what audism does is to colonize the deaf community, but this mystification can be hard to see for those living under the influence of audist ideologies. Audism, coined by Humphries (1975), is akin to ableism, racism, sexism, and other terms referring to the subjugation of people based on privileging one form of knowledge and being over another. Bauman (2004) examines this phenomenon from a metaphysical perspective: "Phonocentrism provides an overriding orientation in which the systems of advantage (education and medicine) form and consolidate power by enforcing a normalcy that privileges speech over sign and hearing over deafness" (p. 245). Audism is present in the lives of children with deafness from multiple fronts, exercising sheer power through rehabilitative projects (for individual) and policy reforms (of institutions) under the impression that deafness needs to be cured.

Now, after writing these stories, I have a new view of what being a robot and a superhero meant and means to me. I understand how I and my family interpellated audism and ableism, allowing the phonocentric and ableist power/knowledge system to colonize our thoughts and our lexicon. Holland and Lave (2001) observe that "social agents, their interactions in practice, their identities, their life trajectories, and their changing understandings" all aid in the "cultural production of identities" (pp. 7-8). Talking and writing about these memories empowers me to reconcile past feelings of alienation, stigma, and failure into feelings of acceptance, pride, and possibility by effectively (re)creating the genealogy and anatomy of my life history, (re)naming and (re)conceptualizing stories with my current subaltern identity.

In an interview, Joe Tobin, talks with me about my evolving subaltern self-concept and identity, interestingly, using the metaphor of superhero to mean something entirely different from the way superhero was constructed by my memory of the playground incident. When I ask Joe how he thought my growing up with deafness informs who I am today, he says, "You had on this...one level, experience of being mistreated...you learned as a subaltern, a perspective that comes from suffering, being marginalized, the costs of passing, you learned to code switch. It gave you determination, gave you high expectations for yourself...you turned disadvantages into strengths. I guess I see you as someone who developed superhero powers, like the comic book hero Daredevil, who goes blind and then develops super senses and becomes a superhero...I see you training for years like that hero, training to develop your senses to become empowered...to make yourself into a Deaf superhero...And in a small way I like to think that I helped you...like Yoda did for Luke Skywalker...My ambition for you is to fight back against the forces of Darkness."

Listening to Joe speak about the metaphor of the superhero (and of me in Star Wars cosmology not as R2D2 but as Luke Skywalker) seems especially odd, considering he never knew about my mother's interview. The theme of superhero cycles back, and this time the word gets (re)defined and a new memory is born. The construction of me as a superhero, having trained under an audist regime to be ready to battle oppression, offers the possibility of taking my internalized experiences of alienation, stigma, and failure and turning them upside down, by assuming a new identity. I see this superhero version of myself as a strategy in the tradition of counter-discourses and counter-storytelling used by oppressed communities (Delgado and Stefancic, 2001). It reminds me of another battle that took place on the playground, again decades ago, but this time with a different outcome; it was the first time I resisted the label "deaf and dumb," battling physically and emotionally to develop my self concept and identity.

ELEVEN

Surfing Hurricane Gloria and the Award-Winning Story

When Hurricane Gloria hits the coast, I can see I'm too far out in the Atlantic Ocean to get back. Everybody else — Sean, Fat Albert, Commander, and Ritchie Rich are safe on the beach. I should have come back to the shore when they first waved for me to. I realize now they were probably warning me about the storm getting worse. I didn't hear them. Sean has my hearing aid in his pocket because I can't get those wet. The waves launch high overhead and crash on top of me. Over and over again, the waves dunk me underwater. I start to worry I will soon be underwater for good.

Finally the motion from the waves bobs me back up to the surface. I start to float some. I can see the black clouds above and the dark choppy waters. I bob up and down a bit in the wave; up and down and up and down. I can feel my surfboard slip out some from underneath me. I scurry back onto it. Every time I go under, it's the board that brings me. I keep holding it close to me, hoping it will keep me afloat. Even though it's drowning me. I wonder if I should just ditch the board and swim as best as I can for shore. I'm a super swimmer and even won a swimming contest at Bayport Beach. I always have been a good swimmer since I went to swimming lessons at Mrs. Reeky's house down the street from ours.

Mrs. Reeky always screamed across the pool, Kick! Kick! Kick!

I can't kick now. The surfboard is tethered to my wrist on a Velcro strap so I just hang on as best I can. Each wave throws me off balance, off the board, and back into the Atlantic. This keeps happening. I can't paddle on the board with the waves so high and the current keeps pulling me back out to the Atlantic.

I start to think: Just a few hours ago I was home with Mom, Poppy, Nanny, baby sister Jill, my older brother John, cousins — Zed, Zeke, and Zen, Aunt Edie and Uncle Stevey, Taby and Toby and their parents, Mr. and Mrs. Oilman. But I wanted to surf Hurricane Gloria because all the kids on the block were talking about it.

Commander invited Fat Albert, Sean, and a few other kids from the neighborhood to borrow his surfboards to go surfing during the hurricane. So everybody stashed them away on the side of Commander's house before our parents made us come home and hunker down for the worst part of the storm. I wasn't invited to surf but I showed up anyway at the appointed time of 3 o'clock. When I get there, I find out two of the boys didn't show and there are two extra boards. I'm not sure if I should ask if I can borrow a board or just say nothing and tag along with it.

Commander sees me standing by the side of the house next to Sean. He says something, but I can't read his lips because he's not facing me all the way and the wind keeps making my hearing aid whistle.

I look to Sean to translate. Sean doesn't translate, just nods his head up and down and gives me the emergency look like say, Yes!

I say, Yes! But I don't know what to.

Commander realizes I didn't hear him. His temper shows some. I'm afraid he won't let me come if I don't hear him right.

Commander gets in my face real close, like I read eyes not lips, and he says, Deaf kid, listen, Little Johnny and Davey musta wimp'd out. If yu wanna to come, yu can. Get a board befor' I change my mind.

I don't say anything except, K. Got it.

I'm so glad. Commander must be in a good mood.

Five of us — Sean, Fat Albert, Commander, Ritchie Rich who is really poor, and me walk down the street to the Great South Bay docks and borrow a row boat parked on the sand near the beach. We row over to Fire Island about a quarter mile away. Commander stands with one leg resting on the bow of the boat, he yells every so often, Row, Row, Row.

Now I sit there in the water and think if I had stayed home, I'd be listening to the weather updates from WBLI on Poppy's battery-operated radio. I love that radio even though I can't make out what people say on it. I love it because John, my older brother and I saved up and bought it for Poppy for his birthday from Crazy Eddie's electronic store. Poppy loves his radio.

Sitting there in the water, I think: Why did I have to sneak out? I bob in the water replaying in my mind sneaking out the basement window from the back by the workshop; using the table saw to hop up and out of the window; leaving the window slightly ajar so I could slip back in later. When I snuck off, all the kids were playing Monopoly and the adults were listening to WBLI, napping, or talking and talking and talking. It was like a party for adults and kids. Everybody was having a good time.

We have the biggest basement so Mom invited everybody to come over. Poppy and Nanny brought all the emergency supplies, even the things none of us would have ever thought of like candles, band-aids, a generator — that we can't use unless we are without electricity for more than a day — and many other cool things like rope, flares, and ten-packs of Wrigley's Spearmint bubble gum. When I snuck out I took a piece of rope, one flare from the box, and one pack of Wrigley's.

Sitting there in the water, I remember the flare. I feel down my leg to see if the flare that I tied with the rope is still there. I reach down some, fumbling around my ankles because I can feel the rope. My fingers finally grab onto the flare and I pull it up above my head. I keep hoping it is waterproof. I try to look at the flare but it's dark and the waves keep bouncing me off my surfboard and I keep trying to get back on. Off to the side standing at the end of the beach, I can see Commander, Fat Albert, Sean, and Ritchie Rich. I can't make out what they are screaming. But I can see that they are screaming.

When I do get a good look at the flare, I see it has a cap. It looks like it is a road flare. Useless in the water I'm guessing. So I pull off the cap, hoping it works. Nothing happens. The flare is dead. I think to myself: Crap.

I wish I had my cape. If I had my cape, I could fly out of here.

I start to think about Death. I don't want to die. I'm too young. I've got to have my superpowers. I've got to find my superpowers. I've just got to. I wish I didn't leave my cape at home. I *need* my cape now.

What would Superman do? Batman? Spiderman? What would they do?

Finally it comes to me: let go of the surfboard, be brave, and superswim. So I undo the Velcro at my ankle. The surfboard takes off with a wave fast. It's gone in seconds. Suddenly I feel so much lighter but now I'm going up and down with the waves. It feels weird. I feel naked against the water.

For a few seconds, I let myself get used to the water without the board. Then I dive into the wave ahead of me. I thrust my arms and legs as hard as I can, even as the current forces me back. I redouble my thrusts. I can feel the burning sensation in my exhausted arms. But my legs feel fine so I use them to power me more. I kick and kick my legs and use my hands and arms to keep me going in the right direction. As long as I can stay underwater I can make headway, I keep telling myself. Every time I come up for air, I look around to be sure I am heading toward the beach. Each time, I have to slow down to a bob and force myself underwater again to press on to the beachhead. I do this every two or three minutes or so, timing it with when I need to come up for air.

When I can't make out Sean or Fat Albert or Commander or Ritchie Rich on the beach anymore, I start to really worry. I wonder if they left to go and get some help. I dive down and keep swimming underwater. I'm not sure if I'm making any headway. I begin to wonder if I'm even swimming in the right direction. The darker it gets, the harder it gets to see. All that I have are the lights from a lone house along the beach. I keep swimming for what seems like hours.

Finally at one point, I come up for air and to see if I am closing in on the beach. When I look up it is all black with the waves being too high to even see over them. It's all just plain dark. I can't even see if I'm even going in the right direction. I get pissed off and scream curses into the wind. The water bobs me up and down.

Damn it. Damn it. Damn it.

I'm so tired. I'm so afraid to admit maybe I just don't want to swim anymore. I wonder if I should quit.

All of a sudden I hear a siren off in the distance. It's not like a police or fire truck siren. It's more like a horn siren. I start to wonder if maybe there is a Coast Guard ship out there. I start to panic maybe I swam the wrong way and I'm even further from shore than I was before. If it were a Coast Guard ship, they would have their floodlights on. I know that for sure. So it can't be them.

I sit in the darkness and try to listen for the siren again. I hear nothing. I can see nothing. I sit and bob, up and down. Up and down. Darkness. Silence. Everything is still. It seems the eye of the storm has passed. There is a gentle calm. I can see black cloud movement above. No stars or moon yet. But I can see the clouds, outlines with thick, darker lines that show the shapes of what looks like black cotton balls. The clouds move fast.

The waves move fast too. The siren sound must have been in my imagination, I think to myself. So I give up listening for it, even though it rings in my ears and in my head. I dive deep down below, this time I don't even know what direction I'm going in. I could be swimming more out to sea. Or I could be swimming to the ocean floor. I lose all sense of direction. All I do is keep kicking my feet, thinking of my swim teacher, Mrs. Reeky, Kick, kick, kick!

I kick my legs as hard as I can. I'm not sure which way is up. I start to panic. I worry I was too rash. I start paddling my feet furiously, imagining myself about to drown when finally I hit my face hard into a rock. I scratch my nose hard. Or did I hit the ocean floor?

I become a bit confused. I grab for whatever it is that is in front of me, letting out the last bit of air I'd saved in my lungs. Bubbles float upward. I can feel something with an edge and it is both a rock and the ocean floor and broken seashells. My hands move frantically about, getting cut by the sharp shells. I keep trying to reach for something that doesn't hurt. I panic some more. Bubbles.

Whatever it is my knees hit it hard too. Finally I realize it is land. It's the beachhead. I made it. I crawl onto the beach. My knees and palms are all scratched up. The closer I crawl onto the beach, the softer the wet sand feels under me. When the sand feels dry, I let myself fall into the ground. I rest. I could sleep forever here. And, for a while I do.

I wake up to Sean shaking me. I open my eyes and it is still dark out. But I can make out Sean's face. He's saying something and keeps shaking me.

Joey, wake up, Sean yells.

When I come to, I realize he is yelling into my face. It takes some time to process it for some reason. It was like I could hear him but I couldn't. When I realize from the look on his face he is yelling, I look at him, say, Hey, stop yellin', I'm awake.

Sean hands me my hearing aid from his pocket, I put the soft piece in my ear canal and the hard piece behind my ears, and he talks in a calmer tone this time, Man, oh, man, I thought yu were dead. Man, oh, man. We all thought yu were dead.

Commander leans over me, talks all sweet and nice-like, Hey, Joey. You not deaf still 're yu?

What, I ask?

Commander repeats, You not deaf still 're yu?

I look at him and Sean. I don't know what to answer back. I nod my head, No, yes.

Commander then leans into my face, Git the hell up, Deaf kid!

Then he does something I never thought Commander would ever do. He gets down to one knee, steadies himself, and offers his hand to pull me up. I'm not sure what to do. Is this a joke?

Is he going to hold my hand and punch me in the face? I don't want to turn down this offer of a truce. No matter what the circumstance is, I want to take advantage of any goodwill I can get from Commander. Even at the risk of being duped and punched.

So I close my eyes, brace for the punch in the face, and give him my hand, squinting my eyes open to look up not at Commander but Sean and Fat Albert, finally Ritchie Rich. They all look at me with their mouths agape. No one says anything.

Commander helps me up. Looks at me and says, Shit, if yu wulda died, my Dad wulda kick'd my ass. Then I wulda hada beat the shit out of yur deaf, dead body. Good thing dis all work'd out fur the best fur all us. Deaf kid, yu sure 're a dumbass.

Right then and there I'm not really sure what to make of what he's saying. Is it good or bad? I wasn't really sure. I did know for sure he wasn't screaming at me, punching me, or in any way bullying me. I liked that. So I figure: whatever. I just smile at him and everybody else. I don't say anything because I don't want ruin this.

We start walking off the beach toward the boardwalk; it's lit up with a few light posts a few hundred yards away. Sean and Fat Albert dust off the sand from my body. Ritchie Rich and Commander are walking a bit ahead of us. It's then that Sean and Fat Albert both realize that I'm naked.

Right after Sean's hand brushes up against my naked butt he screams, Holy shit. Are you frick'n naked?

Commander is talking with Ritchie Rich and looks back at me in the dark but doesn't stop walking. I can almost see the disgust on his face. I make out the first part of what he says, Deaf kid, yu f'ckin kidd'n me? Yu nak'd?

The last part I don't hear. I don't want to know anyway.

Fat Albert jumps in, saves the day, Thank God he's alive. Do yu know how much trubble we'd all be in right now if Joey were dead? His Mom wuld be so pissed at us.

Sean chimes in, Yea, she a crazy, scary Irish redhead too.

Fat Albert adds, Yea, Commander, haha...if Joey were dead his Mom wuld kick ur ass. Hahaha...

Commander says something else but I can't hear him. The wind is blowing hard again and my hearing aid whistles. I can't hear anything the whole way to the boat because the wind keeps blowing into my hearing aid. I can see everybody is laughing. I don't want to ask what they're saying because it's fun to be hanging out with the older kids on the block.

We get to the rowboat on the other side of Fire Island and take off for Bayport just across the Bay. The whole ride across the Bay, Fat Albert cracks jokes about my mom being a World Wrestling Federation champion fighter. Ritchie Rich just laughs, nods his head, laughs some more – he is not afraid of anybody or anything because he is a better fighter than everybody on the block. One time Ritchie Rich even beat up Commander when Commander told him to shut-up at the Big Tree House in the woods. No one tells Ritchie Rich to shut-up, not even Commander. But usually Ritchie Rich just loves to laugh. So the whole boat ride back he cracks up at anything anyone says.

In the boat, Fat Albert looks to Sean and me to see if Commander is going to go off the deep end or stay cool with his jokes. You never know with Commander. Right now he seems chill so Fat Albert goes on with his comedy routine.

Fat Albert keeps going on about how my mom would kick Commander's ass, then my mom would kick Commanders' mom's ass, and then everybody jumped in to argue whether my mom could fight Commander's dad, Mr. Commander, if he is a man and my mom is a woman. There had to be some rule about men and women fighting we argued. Commander doesn't really say anything but he doesn't look annoyed by any of this anyway. He seems to be thinking of something, alone in his thoughts.

We finally land ashore on Long Island, prop the boat up against the dock, and walk home in the driving rain, leftover from the passing Hurricane Gloria. It takes about a half hour or so to walk to the end of Bayport Avenue, where we all live. First we stop by Commander's house to drop off the surfboards. I don't have mine. Commander doesn't say anything so I don't remind him my board is lost forever. We all say good-bye at Commander's house and take off for home. Fat Albert runs off, waving and screaming, Later!

Ritchie Rich and Commander disappear into his backyard.

Sean looks at me, Man, that was crazy, hu?

We walk slowly toward his house; my house is just three houses up the street. I look down and see a firework shooter's dream just lying in the middle of street, across the way from Sean's place. I reach down and pick it up to show him.

He says, Wow. Awesome, a M-80.

I look at the M-80, and then Sean and say, I hope this works.

I go on, I can get some of Poppy's flares and if this works, we can blow the crap outta Commander and those guys in the Bottle Rocket Wars. That would be awesome!

Sean's smiling. I'm smiling. We walk along, single-file, balancing on the curb with me leading the way. We both use our arms as wings to balance. The rain comes down hard and the wind makes it more of a challenge than usual.

I look at Sean, Yea. Now all we need to do is sneak back into the house.

With the M-80 too, he says.

Yea, I look behind me, I'll put it on the side of my house by the garbage. I'm the one who has to always take it out so no one will see it there.

Sean says, Yea. Good idea, Joey.

We stop on the sidewalk in front of his house. The rain doesn't look like it's going to let up anytime soon. Even though neither of us is saying it, we don't want to go home yet because sneaking back in is going to be tough. That's if our parents don't already know.

Just then, Sean's dad, Mr. O'McFinley comes running out of his house. His face looks *pissed*.

He yells to us both, Get in here! We've been looking all over for you two.

Sean and I look at one another. We both have panic all over our faces. The panic strikes me double-time when I see Mom walk out of Mr. O'McFinley's house. My mom was at Sean's?

Now I know this means I'm in really big trouble. It's seems odd to watch Mom run across Sean's yard. I've never seen Mom run before. I can see she has really bad form. I never could figure out where I got my athletic genes. It must have passed generations because John wasn't much of an athlete either. I don't know why I was thinking this at that moment. Just a random thought, I guess. But I'd rather think about that than what is about to happen.

When Mom starts hugging me *and* screaming at me, things get more odd. It's like she is mad and happy to see me at the same time.

Mom looks down at me, What is that?

I look up at her, What?

The rain falls down hard on us both. Mom's soaked.

Mr. O'McFinley yells for us from under his porch, Come on, it's raining and lightning. Get in the house.

Mom grabs the M-80 out of my hand, gives me the Look, and takes my hand to run back to Mr. O'McFinley's house. Mrs. O'McFinley is standing there with Sean's sister, Bridget. I have a crush on Sean's little sister, Bridget, and hope she is going to be my girlfriend someday when we're old enough to date and marry. Both Mrs. O'McFinley and Bridget have a bath towel in each hand for us both. I take the towel from Bridget, try to look cool giving her a wink for 'hello', and dry off my head. It is then that I remember I'm naked. I stop drying myself and just use the towel to cover up my privates.

Heya, Bridge, I say.

Bridget says nothing, except a weak, Yur nak'd, Joey. Her thick glasses are all fogged up.

Mom looks to her and then me. She sees I'm just standing there not doing anything and takes the bath towel away from me, drying my head and body herself.

Mom is rough, toweling my head and thrusting me about. I get testy at Mom because she is making me look like a little kid around Bridget. Mom knows I like her because she helps me make the secret Valentine's Day cards I send to Bridget every year.

When Mom is done, Mrs. O'McFinley tells me to go to the upstairs bathroom where she laid out some dry clothes I can borrow from Sean. She tells Mom there is a dry sweatsuit waiting for her in the downstairs bathroom. Mrs. O'McFinley takes Mom to the bathroom leading the way with a flashlight because she is worried Mom will fall. Mom tells her not to bother. But Mrs. O'McFinley doesn't listen. Instead she tells Mr. O'McFinley and Sean to use the other flashlight and take me upstairs.

Bridget just disappears around the staircase.

In the bathroom, I put on Sean's jogging pants and sweatshirt. It feels good to be dry and warm. I sit on the toilet wishing I didn't have to leave. I know once I get out there Mom is going to give me the Look several times. She won't yell at me in front of the O'McFinleys but she will when we get home. Until then, Mom will just throw the Look at me. I'm never sure what is worse — the Look and waiting for punishment or the getting yelled at and the punishment.

I come out of the bathroom when the electricity comes on. All the lights in the house are on and I can hear a radio and television going on too. It's so weird when everything lights back up and the electronics come back to life.

Mrs. O'McFinley hands Mom a cup of coffee, no sugar, only half and half. Mom can never turn down a cup of coffee so she sits down and starts chatting with Sean's parents. They tell her about how they got their pool specially cleaned for the winter. Mom thanks them for being so nice, chats about pools being so expensive, and puts on her phony sweet voice, where she exaggerates all her words and that she is interested in what they're saying: "Oh, reeeeeaaaalllly" "Ohh, Thaaaat's soooo exciting" "Do—not—saaaaay." It all just comes off phony, I think. But all adults seem to like talking like that to each other.

The television is also blaring about a Coast Guard search going on for a missing surfer right now. So Mrs. O'McFinley tells Sean to turn it down so they can hear each other better. When he does, Mom remembers the M-80 and pulls it out of her pocket.

Mom says, What's this?

I look at her, It's a M-80 firecracker.

Why do you have this?

I found it.

Where?

In the street.

Really? Mom looks at me. She thinks I'm lying.

Mom asks, You didn't buy this for the Bottle Rocket Wars?

No.

Really? She says. Clearly she doesn't believe me.

Mom looks at Mr. and Mrs. O'McFinley, then she looks at Sean and me, You two weren't off shooting firecrackers in the storm?

No, we both nod our heads up and down in unison.

Mr. O'McFinley fidgets in his seat. He's itching to smack Sean's ass. I know it because whenever he is about to, he starts to tap his leg like he is warming up. He doesn't reach for Sean because Sean moves closer to his mother, his human shield. I'm betting Mr. O'McFinley won't smack him if he is near his mom.

Sean doesn't say anything. As always he freezes. So it's up to me to defend us.

I say, Me and Sean, we weren't shootn' crackers, Mom, I promise. We were just walking around the neighborhood.

Mom and Mr. and Mrs. O'McFinley aren't buying our story. They say so.

Lying is only going to get you in more trouble, Mom says, What happened to your clothes?

Sean freezes. He'll let me answer that question. Mrs. O'McFinley saves us.

Sean, Mrs. O'McFinley says, Answer Mrs. Valente truthfully. What were you two doing? Who were you two with? Commander? Fat Albert? Little Johnny? Freckles? Ritchie Rich?

I look at Sean. I try to tell him telepathically to shut up, to not bring Commander into this or we're going to have more trouble on our hands.

True to his word, Sean says nothing, again. He stays quiet.

So I speak up, No, no, no one was with us. It was just us. We walked the neighborhood.

Mom looks at me, Fine, I'll just call all their parents tomorrow to see if they were home during the storm. It's hard to believe you two when you don't always tell the truth.

Mom is now angry at us for not just confessing.

Mr. O'McFinley looks at Sean, You better be telling the truth or you're going to wish you did. The two of you could have been hurt wandering around the street, shooting those stupid firecrackers off. So you better be telling the truth or else.

Sean just gives me the look like I just handed him a life sentence.

I give him the look back like I've got everything under control. But I can see he's not buying it.

Mom looks at me, she says, I don't need to wait to find out if you are telling the truth. You are already grounded for having this firecracker in your hand and running around the neighborhood naked during a hurricane. What is it with you? How do you come up with this stuff?

She goes on, If I find out you're lying, then you'll just be grounded longer. Now let's go so Mr. and Mrs. O'McFinley can get some peace and quiet around here.

Oh, you're not any trouble, Mrs. O'McFinley, says but stands up and walks us to the door anyway.

Mom says, You're too kind. Come on, Joey. The storm has died down some. Let's get home. Nanny and Poppy and everyone else is probably worried sick about the both of us by now.

I say good-bye to Sean. Mom and I walk the three houses down to our house.

When we get home, everybody is sitting around the television watching the news. Nobody seems to care that I was gone, except Nanny who wants to know what happened. I say nothing so Nanny knows to let it go until later when Mom isn't around. I always tell Nanny everything because she doesn't tell Mom on me.

Everybody's attention is on the television now. The TV set shows a Coast Guard helicopter hovering around the Fire Island beach area, off the Atlantic Ocean, so everyone is watching to see if the lost person at sea is someone we all might know. The news reporter on the scene explains that a Coast Guard Cutter had been at sea during the storm and had seen someone holding onto a surfboard. But they could not make the person out because the spotlight used for searches had been destroyed during the Hurricane by a strike of lightning. The reporter announces that the Coast Guard suspects the surfer may have not made it because someone recovered a surfboard on the beach just minutes ago. But no body washed ashore yet.

It is then that it occurs to me, maybe, what they found was my surfboard. Maybe it was me they were talking about.

I want to turn to Mom and tell her but I'm afraid I'll get in more trouble now. I don't even know if she would even believe me because I've told so many stories already. I feel bad that those Coast Guard sailors have to be at Ocean. I'm not sure what to do.

Our phone rings and Mom answers it. She says, Joey, it's Sean.

Before she hands me the phone, she says to Sean, Enjoy this conversation because once Joey's grounding starts, the phone is off limits, even between you two. You'll both need to get some cans and string if you want to talk long-distance now.

OK, Mrs. Valente. Thank you, Sean says. He is such a kiss-ass.

Mom hands me the phone.

Before I take it, I ask her, How long am I grounded?

You're grounded for eternity, Mom says.

I laugh and say, Sure Mom.

I take my hearing aid out so it doesn't whistle against the receiver, get on the phone with Sean and he says, Holy Macaroni. Did yu see the TV?

Yea, I say.

Wha jwuldo?

Hu? I ask.

What...

...should...

...we do? Sean asks again slowly. He's panicked again.

Say nothing, I say.

What? Sean says.

I said, say nothing, Sean. Do you want to get in more trouble?

No, he says.

Alright? I say.

OK, he says.

Hu? I ask.

OK, I said, Sean repeats himself. He doesn't ever get mad if I don't hear him.

Alright, see you tomorrow.

OK, he says.

We hang up. Sean knows I'm not a big phone talker.

Everybody leaves after the news show ends because it's getting real late now. Taby and Toby and their parents, my cousins, aunt and uncle, and everybody says, Good-bye.

Nanny and Poppy plan to spend the night. Soon Mom makes John and me go to bed. Baby Jill has been sleepy all day and is already asleep. Lying in bed, I look out the window. I can't help but wonder if the Coast Guard boats are still out there, looking for me. I feel bad. I want to tell somebody but I can't because I will get into trouble and no one will believe me anyway.

I sit there in bed, feeling really tired and sleepy; I look out the window, watching the clouds pass over the stars. I fall into a deep sleep with dreams of Coast Guard ships, the high seas, and me just so tired from swimming. In the morning when I wake, I realize those weren't dreams. No, they were nightmares.

A few days go by and school is out because there are live telephone wires down all over the neighborhood. No one is allowed to drive or go anywhere. It doesn't matter because I'm grounded. John gets to go over his friend's house, just a few houses down the street because it is safe. Jill is more interested in playing with her dolls and coloring books than entertaining me. Mom has to go to work because she's a nurse. Nanny has to stay with me the whole time, making sure I don't watch TV. She sits with me and tells me about growing up on Long Island, being the daughter of a duck farmer, and what is was like around these neighborhoods out East. I listen because Nanny tells really interesting history stories and even shows me cool things like ration cards from World War II and pictures of her family duck farm and Poppy in his uniform at the end of The War. Nanny even shows me pictures of Mom and herself when they looked like movie stars. I get to learn about how things used to be. Nanny tells me about how our family came over from the old country to the City and how we came from the City to Long Island. Everybody did it like that she said.

All Long Islanders have roots in the City, she tells me.

Nanny has to clean, do some laundry, and get dinner ready. She's making baked ziti with Ragu sauce but we can't tell Mom it's from a jar and not made from scratch.

Nanny says, It's our little secret, right?

Uh-hu, I say. Nanny and me have many little secrets.

I have to stay at the kitchen table. Nanny says, Why don't you read a book?

I don't feel like reading a book at the table. I like to read on the couch or in bed.

I say, Nah, I don't feel like it.

She says, Well, then write a story.

OK, I say.

So I write a story about me drowning in the Ocean and the Coast Guard comes and rescues me and I get to be on television and then I become a movie star. Nanny loves the story.

Nanny says, Maybe you'll be in a movie with Marlon Brando.

Nah, I say. Not Brando, Nanny.

Well, who then?

James Dean, Nanny. James Dean is cool.

Nanny laughs and says, Well, that might be tough to do.

Why? I ask.

Because he's not alive no more, Nanny says.

Oh, I say, How about Jackie Gleason?

Nanny says, I'm not sure if he's alive no more. She laughs, says, Good story, Joey. Nanny pats me on the head, says it again, Good story. Keep writing. Bring it to school and show that teacher you like so much.

I look at her and say, Mrs. Kapell?

Yes, she says, Show her.

The first day back to school after Hurricane Gloria, I take the story to school to show Mrs. Kapell. I take it to her first thing in the morning. I'm sure to arrive a little early before school starts. Even though they won't let us past a certain point in the lobby that leads to the classrooms, I try to figure out a way to see Mrs. Kapell anyway.

I walk into the office and say, Hi, to all the secretaries working there.

They all know me. I'm hoping Mrs. Kapell might come by and get her mail so I sit on the chair that I have to sit on when I visit Mr. Weik, the principal, when I'm in trouble. It's nice to get to sit there this time and not be in trouble. The secretaries want to know why I have to wait.

I explain: I have a story I have to share with Mrs. Kapell. It's really important.

That nice old church lady secretary who goes to the same 5 o'clock Mass we go to on Saturday seems to want to know about this story, she asks me, What's the story about?

I tell her, It's about me. I become a movie star because they found me on CBS News after being rescued by the Coast Guard and Hollywood thought I was too good to pass up.

The old church lady says, Interesting.

But she doesn't look interested.

Hold on, she says.

The old lady secretary gets on the phone, turns the dial three times, talks for a bit, laughs, and gets off the phone.

The old lady says, Go on down to Mrs. Kapell's room, she said you could come early.

I jump up from my chair and hurry out into the lobby and head for the hallway. The Captain of the Safety Team, Gary, stands guard in front of a red rope that is tied to a stand on each side, it's to block entrance into the hallway.

The Captain says, Hey you, you can't go in here.

He blocks me so I can't go down the hallway.

I say, Hey, Captain Gary, the Office called Mrs. Kapell. I can go down here. I have permission.

He gets on his walkie-talkie and says into it: Gary, here.

The walkie-talkie gives a static bark back: Mrs. Gran-spaghetti, 'er.

Mrs. Grambetti, that Deaf kid 'er, saying he got a pass to Mrs. K.

Walkie-talkie: Gary, don't say that in front of him. That's not nice. Did he hear that?

He looks at me and asks, Did yu hear that?

Hear what? I ask.

He speaks back into the walkie-talkie: Mrs. Grambetti he didn't hear nutn'.

OK, she says, Let him go to Mrs. K's.

Captain Gary unclicks the latch on the rope and gives me enough room to get through before clasping it back onto the stand. I walk really quickly down the hallway with the story about my Coast Guard rescue and movie career in my hand. I wish I could run but Captain Gary would give me a running ticket. I don't want to get one, not now.

When I get to Mrs. Kapell's room, I show her the story.

Mrs. Kapell reads it and says, Wow.

I ask her, What do yu think?

Mrs. Kapell says, This is quite a story, Joey. How did you think of this?

I wrote it during Hurricane Gloria, I say.

Wow. She really, really looks impressed.

You really have an amazing imagination, Joey, she says.

I say, Thanks, Mrs. Kapell.

She seems real proud of that story, looks at me, asks, What do you want to do with this story?

I want to make it a book, I say.

Oh, she says, How do we do that?

We should type it up, I say.

Alright, let's go do it, she says.

Let's go see if Mrs. Grambetti will let us use her typewriter or tell us where we can get one, Mrs. Kapell says.

Together we walk down the hallway to the office. When we get to the ropes and Captain Gary, he doesn't ask her for a pass or anything. That must be nice. I can't wait to be a grown-up and walk anywhere I want to.

We go into the office and I sit on that chair again.

Mrs. Kapell comes back and says Mrs. Grambetti will let us borrow a portable typewriter. So we bring it back to Mrs. Kapell's room and she helps me type it all up. When I'm done, I make a cover, drawing a picture of the town of Bayport like an old-fashioned treasure map. I even tear the sides of the paper some to make the map look old. I use this as the cover for my story.

When I'm done Mrs. Kapell says, Can I hold onto the story for a bit. I want to share it with some of the teachers.

I say, OK.

A few days later we have a school assembly. Mr. Weik calls me up to the podium. But I don't hear him. Sean, sitting next to me, pokes me.

Joey, Sean says, Mr. Weik is calling yur name.

Oh, I say.

I get up quick and run the three steps up to the stage. Mr. Weik leans down from the podium and hands me a piece of paper.

I stand there next to him as he says, Everyone please give Joey Valente a round of applause. He's won an award for the best story of the school year. Good job, Joey.

Mrs. Kapell stands over in the corner by the stage, smiling proud. I'm so excited I run all the way home to give Mom the golden paper with my name in calligraphy. Mom puts it on the fridge and we go out to dinner at my favorite Mexican restaurant, Chi-Chi's, to celebrate with chicken chimichangas and fried ice cream.

TWELVE

"And no more deaf and dumb jokes"

I'm on the handball court playing a quick round before school starts with my best friend, Sean. We're both in the same third-grade class with Mrs. Conklin. We walk to school together every day and play after school all the time. When I'm about to serve the ball, the school-bully known by his last name, Puck, comes up to me from behind and says, "Deaf boy! Gimme the ball."

I don't hear him at first; eyeing the box painted white on the brick school wall, I bounce the blue ball with my serving-hand. Noticing Sean's eyes widening, I turn around. Puck stands right behind me, now yelling directly into my hearing aid, "Deaf boy! Gimme the ball." I'm about to wet myself in fear, and he pushes me to the ground. The blue ball rolls away.

On my back now, I ask, "What?"

He leans in, inches away from my face, and says to the crowd surrounding us, "'What' is your favorite word, idiot. Now we all know you're deaf and dumb." He laughs, still standing over me, and grabbing my hearing aids out of my ears, says "Then you have no need for these."

I'm boiling inside. I want to kill him, but I know his friends will jump in and help him. He stomps on my hearing aids and I cry, thinking about my mother and what she would say. Earlier this year I had already flushed my hearing aids down the toilet and dived into a pool with them on. I can't lose another hearing aid now.

I sit there on the ground quiet with rage.

Puck just laughs.

People in the crowd around us watch like it is a television show. No one says anything. I sit there hoping someone will tell Puck to pick on someone his own size. No one does. Puck just stands over me like a fighter in a ring, waiting to pounce on me the minute I get up. So I just sit there on the ground in defeat. I wish so badly I could punch him.

Puck says, "Come on, I dare you, get up."

He laughs some more and finally the morning warning bell rings. Puck and everyone else runs to the open doors. Sean helps me up, handing me my hearing aids. I'm so relieved when I see that they are not broken. Puck must have just pretended to crush them but only placed his foot on them instead. I still want to punch him.

Instead of going to Mrs. Conklin's class like I'm supposed to, I walk directly to my speech pathologist Mrs. Kapell's room, my second-mother – my haven, and tell her what happened. She is furious; her face looks hurt. I'm beginning to get bullied more frequently now and she worries about me.

Mrs. Kapell hugs me, and I ask her what I should do and she says, "What do you think you should do?"

"Beat him up, but I will get in trouble," I say.

"Joey, there is a difference between fighting and defending yourself. You are allowed to defend yourself," she says.

I'm shocked because I thought she would have been mad at me for fighting no matter what. Before sending me on my way with a late-note, Mrs. Kapell tells me she has a surprise for me, "It is an attaché case." She shows me how to work the code to unlock it. I feel, suddenly, like a real writer now. I'm so excited and thank her with a big hug. I put my lunch inside and take it with me to class.

When I get back up to class, Mrs. Conklin is helping my classmates with something over at the project area so I just go to my desk. Sean comes over and asks, "You okay?"

"Yes," I tell him.

"Did Puck call you out?"

"You mean did he call me out to fight?"

"Yea," Sean looks at me.

"No, Puck didn't say he called me out. I didn't hear him say that. Did you?"

"No," Sean says. But I can tell he's not too sure.

"Well, if he did, I'm goin' to fight him." I put on a brave face.

"Get out," Sean says.

"No, I will. I'm going to really punch him hard. I'm going to make him cry."

"Get out. Well, he didn't give you a time, right?"

"What do you mean?"

"You know, if he says: I call you out for after school. Then he sets a time. You have to be there for that time. So you can fight."

"Oh."

"But I don't remember him setting a time so I don't think he called you out."

As fate would have it, after school that day I was walking home alone. Sean had band practice so he couldn't walk home with me like we usually do. Taking a shortcut through a small wooded area near the school, I see Puck walking in the opposite direction on the path alone. He sees me and yells, "Oh, you want me to kick your ass again."

I'm not as nervous this time because he is alone and I'm allowed to defend myself. He approaches me and pushes me back a little. I let the anger inside build up. Before he pushes me again, I swing my fist right into his eye socket harder than I ever hit my brother, John. He falls backwards on his rear-end, crying. I'm totally surprised by my perfectly landed punch and his tears. He gets up to throw another punch and hits me square in the chest. I knee him in the gut as we both fall to the ground. We are both screaming and rolling around on the earth. I finally end up on top, pinning his arms down, I land a few punches at his head. He bawls and screams for me to let him up, so I do. But not before I say, "You better leave me alone from now on."

He says, "Yes, just get off me."

I add, "And no more deaf and dumb jokes."

THIRTEEN

Un/Learning d/Deaf and d/Dumb

This is not the last time I had to defend myself physically; unfortunately, it is one of many fights I had in school. But it was the first time I stood up for myself. It was the first time I realized I did not deserve to be treated so hurtfully. I did not deserve to be punished for being different. Foucault (e.g., 1978, 1992, 1995) tells us that our bodies are a battlefield that forces us to navigate the binary fields determined by normative power/knowledge constructs. For each child with deafness, they are interpellated by phonocentric ideologies that see difference as pathology. Epistemically violent phonocentrism/audism works to (de)humanize, (ab)normalize, and discipline the always already failing body. In thinking about how the experience of defending myself manifested feelings of empowerment, I realize this was the beginning of my saying no to "deaf and dumb." I wonder how this might reflect who I am today.

Naturally my mother, brother, and sister had different answers. My mom laughs before saying, "You never turn down a fight." John adds, "You were always a pain in the ass, questioning everything, everybody, still do." My younger sister, Jill tells me, "Joey, everyone knows you love to spar verbally, you love pushing people to react." I guess some things never change; I hope this part of me never changes. I'm proud to be an agitator for what I think is right. As a young child I learned to see the world from a marginalized viewpoint. I learned I had to be tough, to fight the forces inside and outside from oppressing me.

According to Katherine Jankowski (1997), "people literally talk their way through life, translating their beliefs into action through such talk," and part of doing this project has been a chance for me to come closer to who I am as a scholar, storyteller, and person (p. 4). For me, the term "deaf and dumb" symbolizes moments in my life, both past and present, where I feel the overwhelming weight of internalized alienation, stigma, and failure. Padden and Humphries (2005) uncover the history of the very Foucauldian "deaf and dumb" in U.S. schools with its genesis dated to the last part of the nineteenth century, defining it as an epistemic and lexical mechanism for silencing people with deafness as "inmates" to be watched, labeled, and prepped for normalization.

Unlearning "deaf and dumb" and claiming my "Deaf-self" is a journey I am still on today. I don't imagine it is a journey with an end; rather, it is a process. This book is a part of the journey; a narrative composed of snapshots of the past seen through new eyes. The unlearning of oppression is a difficult task. Donna Reeve (2002) writes about reclaiming and empowering the disability identity: "The experience of psycho-emotional disablism is not inevitable because disabled people can resist technologies of power imposed from above and may transform themselves by 'coming out' as a disabled person – reclaiming disability as a positive identity" (p. 494). The resistance, though, is a lifelong struggle to externalize internalized oppression through counter-storytelling and other tactics. My story both is and is not my story alone. Children in school today may have stories like and unlike my own, stories we need to give *life to* through *counter life storytelling*.

Counter stories about the lived experiences of people with deafness are bountiful on the worldwide web, where access to multiple mediums such as print and video allow for the diverse language modalities represented in the d/Deaf community. The same could be said about the worldwide web Deafhood discourse community. A web-search reveals www.deafhood.com, a site created to answer Paddy Ladd's (2003) challenge to engage in Deafhood discourse (though as of this writing the site is still under construction); www.deafdc.com designed as forward-looking blogosphere that discusses issues both past and real-time; and other various informative sites such as www.deafhooddiscourses.com (introduces Deafhood concepts); www.ascdeaf.com (parallels feminism with Deafhood); and www.deafread.com (which has an informative blog narrative describing Paddy Ladd's landmark talk about Deafhood at Gallaudet University). On occasions I have engaged in dialogue with d/Deaf bloggers, finding it to be a welcome respite and opportunity to put on my alter-ego as a Deaf subaltern, especially considering my inability to communicate in American Sign Language.

While looking at the popular DeafDC website, I came across a past blog session on "deaf and dumb", and immediately the ethnographer in me went to work looking for stories dis/similar to my own. I did not find stories about feeling "deaf and dumb"; instead I found a discourse on the past and present meaning of "deaf and dumb."

What captivated me the most was a blogger's discussion about the renaming of the term, saying, "Do you think in 50 years from now, the term "Deaf and Dumb" will be in vogue amongst hip deaf crowd? Just like the gay scene embracing the word "queer." Also, the African American community using the n-word as a term of affection."[1] A respondent to this blog forwarded a link to a recent *Time* magazine opinion editorial in opposition to the desire for some to make the "n-word" extinct. Perhaps, without knowing, the blogger on this website was exploring the possibility of counter-dialoguing about and counter-naming "Deaf and Dumb." The blog session shows the blogger's understandings of the painful lineage of the term; yet at the same time the blogger chooses to reown it by liberatory praxis as evidenced by her paralleling "Deaf and Dumb" with the reinvention (though not by everyone in these communities) of "queer" and the "n-word."

For this blogger, the meaning and intent seems to be to compare the ideas behind the taking back of these once marginalizing terms. It is comforting to know that I am not the only one wrestling with the renaming of "deaf and dumb." I want to make it clear that I'm not advocating for the resurgence of the term "deaf and dumb" by the majoritarian society. Though just as equally, I don't want to close the door on the possibility in the future that this term may undergo a transformation akin to the word queer, if people in the d/Deaf community so choose. For now, I'm using the term

---

1   Retrieved March 1, 2008 from http://www.deafdc.com/blog/rob-rice/2006-12-05/about-the-deaf-and-dumb/

metaphorically to explore the spaces that are inevitably created and juxtaposed between the hearing world and d/Deaf world identities, as well as stories of silence versus empowerment.

The genealogy of the term d/Deaf as defined by Woodward (1972) refers to the space(s) between the hearing and visual lifeworlds in which people with deafness live. This/These space(s) are viewed as a continuum, from hearing/speech to visualizing/sign communication modalities, that is largely dependent on (over/under) exposure to oralism or Deaf culture/American Sign Language. The pathway from deaf to Deaf, using this idea of the continuum, also includes an added complexity due to proliferation of varyingly mixed speech/ sign systems such as Signed Exact English (or Signed Essential English), Pidgin Signed English, Signed English, Cued Speech, Simultaneous Communication, Total Communication, and more. My own lifeworld growing up was an example of overexposure to oralism and underexposure to Deaf culture/American Sign Language. Using Woodward's definition, I was raised (oral) deaf. I see now that the word "deaf" in my use of the term d/Deaf and d/Dumb illustrates the irony that I've been silenced not only through the subjugation of schooling and the medical-rehabilitative community but also by not being able to learn American Sign Language. I'm silent in the Deaf-World.

To this day, I feel deeply pained by not having had, what I think, is a fair chance to immerse myself in American Sign Language and the Deaf-World. I lament not learning ASL. But this is not the entire story either (forgive the defensive tone); I've taken three formal ASL classes at different universities and enrolled in multiple community education workshops. The problem, the way I see it, is that I don't function in the Deaf-World enough — yet. These are the costs of growing up oral deaf. I've had to, and I still am on a journey to find my way to the Deaf-World, a common theme and motif in d/Deaf life storytelling. I'm alienated from a community much like people in populations whose communities suffered and are suffering through ethnocides and displacements in the United States.

Let me take a brief sidebar here: Whenever I explain this to people in conversations, time and time again they ask me a variation of this question: If you learned ASL from workshops and classes, why can't you have access to the Deaf community?

This question continuously frustrates me. People who ask this question are not thinking about it practically (so we're now officially moving from the "defensive tone" I mentioned earlier to being fully defensive here). Usually my sharp response and volleys back go something like this:

I grew up in a hearing family and function in the hearing-world. Who am I going to sign with after class? Myself in the mirror?

I never met a Deaf person (or one that I knew was Deaf) until I took an ASL class in college (okay, now that I think about this some more, maybe, I passed another Deaf person in the hall at those audiology clinics or that kid from the playground at preschool but these meetings with Deaf people are simply too infrequent). Only one out of all the ASL classes I had taken was taught by a Deaf person and never was there another Deaf person in any of the classes I was in. One time when I was in college, Joan Kapell offered to pay for me to take an ASL summer course at a local university on Long Island to meet a language requirement for Bates College back in Maine, where I was going to school. She and I talked about me wanting to take ASL over dinner one night and Mrs. Kapell thought it was a great idea. We only briefly talked about the ASL class because I was more interested in catching up. After dinner on the ride home, I was surprised when Mrs. Kapell handed me the money in cash to pay for the class. But that was typical Mrs. Kapell – so sweet and unconditionally loving. I enrolled in the class the very next day. It is there that I met my first Deaf person, who was an ASL professor. I asked her where I could meet Deaf people. She told me to check out a Deaf Night at some bar close to New York City, a long distance away. I drove there anyway. When I went to Deaf Night, I just sat there, trying to finger spell and use the limited ASL I had learned in class. No one seemed to want to chat with me because I really was too slow. I don't blame them. Who wants to chat with someone who can't really do much chatting?

Sometimes, I feel like as a Deaf person, I've failed to thrive.

Yet, again, this is not the entire story. I do have some of the characteristics shared by my Deaf brethren – my visual, even sometimes cinematic, view of the world; even, my in-between-ness, I discovered during my interviews. For every good, there is a bad. While I cherish my visual view of the world, I'm often only "passing" even when people think they are making strides to help me communicate. My family and friends know I need to strategically use my ears and eyes.

My younger sister Jill shares this insight, "You may have been oral deaf but, Joey, you changed the whole family...believe it or not, we care about you," she laughs some, "our whole family speaks so, so loudly. We know there are some places not to go so you can hear us. And, no hands in front of the face! Mom always said. It's like stage acting and direction [having a conversation with me]. I think we are all more animated because we know it adds to your understanding. Now we are all just that way."

I'm thinking to myself that Jill is forgetting that Mom, the matriarch of storytelling with words and body, is also a reason for us all being so animated when we talk.

Jill goes on, "Come on, Joey, don't you think we wanted you to feel like a part of the family?"

"Of course," I say without hesitation.

"You may have been oral deaf, but you were also – I think – sometimes like a big "D" deaf too, everyone around you learns about how you see the world, you change people, the way they talk, the way they act, where they stand when talking," I think Jill is getting at an interesting point, she is referring to how my eyes are an integral part of the way I make sense of the world and how people close to me who understand this adjust and adapt. It never occurred to me that my own way of interacting in the world also is/was interpellated by those in my life, molding not only my identity and our interactions but also shaping those that were close to me. Like me, my family and friends were interpellated by hearing-world ideologies. And like me, sometimes my family and friends accepted these interpellations and sometimes they resisted, and in the process transformed themselves and how we interact.

I now realize how people in my life perceived my residual hearing. Joe Tobin commented on his own experiences interacting with me: "I notice you are more likely with your good friends to say, 'Let's switch sides,' so you can hear them better." This is only partly true. I'm more inclined in academic contexts than in social or public ones to let it be known that I'm Deaf. Even though I'm aware of how the phonocentric world perceives me and I want to resist, sometimes I just think it is easier to "pass" as hearing.

Bob Capuozzo, my good friend and former classmate at Arizona State University, says, "When we walk together, I always go to the side where you can hear me...when people meet you, they don't know you're deaf...you lip-read so well, you pretend to hear well, too," Bob chuckles softly and his voice trails off some, I sense he's reaching back for something in his memory: "For me personally, we met a number of times before I knew you were deaf, it was not until we started hanging out and taking classes together that I realized...no one ever seems to know...and when they do find out, they learn it's a good thing to look at you when talking."

Jill talks about this also, "many people never know that you wear a hearing aid, read lips, and do a lot of guesswork...many times you hide it."

I respond, "I disagree. I don't think I hide it as much as I ignore it."

Jill counters, "No...now you keep your hair short with the hearing aids, but you didn't always, remember? You hid your hearing aids with your longer hair when we were younger. Now you hide it by getting that super small one you got."

Jill's right. I do hide my hearing aid still (I stopped wearing bilaterals long ago). This is one of the quandaries of being so resistant to technology (which I will talk about in great detail later). I appreciate technology giving me the chance to "pass," and not having to explain to the world every day I'm Deaf. Confronting hearing world ideology is a minute-by-minute battle that I often don't want to face.

These are snapshots of the d/Deaf and d/Dumb space. In this way, I use d/Deaf and d/Dumb as a way to describe these moments in my life as spaces that I negotiate and spend my days living, working, and learning. At many points in my life growing up, I thought my hearing aid itself was responsible for this feeling of internalized oppression, the always already failing ear. To me the hearing aid symbolized feelings of silence versus empowerment, tangibly by being my conduit to the outside hearing world, and intangibly through the scripted, sometimes organic, ways my identity and interactions interpellated phonocentrism and my in-between world not just as a d/Deaf person but as a mainstreamed special education student in school.

FOURTEEN

"Your reading scores are at the level of a fifth grader"

It is the fall of 1989, I'm in eighth grade sitting in Mrs. Martin's resource room around a table with my individualized education plan team. My mother can't make the meeting; she's now a single mother and nurse, stuck at the hospital, so Mrs. Martin invites me to come, telling me she thinks it would be good for me to report back to my mother. My English teacher is there, the school psychologist and some other people I do not recognize. They all have folders and papers and I sit there watching them make small talk, waiting on someone to start the meeting. That someone comes in and it's the cool, young assistant principal who I always see in the parking lot with the fancy red convertible sports car, coming late from another meeting.

Mrs. Martin starts by saying how proud of me she is; how far I've come since she started working with me in sixth grade; how "special" I am. I really like her because no matter what, she thinks everyone is exceptional, plus she lets me use my time with her to get homework done. Mrs. Martin actually likes to talk with me, unlike most adults who don't want to talk with adolescents. She looks real old-school in appearance, wearing thick, black pointy glasses that are a holdover from the 1960s. Others around the table join in and start talking about where I will be placed this upcoming school year. Then the conversation shifts to a recent test I took.

Mrs. Martin says, "I think we should add something in the IEP about vocabulary development."

I ask, "Why do we need to do that?"

"Your vocabulary test scores were a little low, so I think it might help if we work on that," Mrs. Martin responds. The people around the table watch.

"How bad were my scores," I ask.

"They were not bad, Joe. We need to work on this a little that's all." Mrs. Martin can see that I'm getting riled.

I feel like everyone else knows something I don't. I look at the papers in front of them, wondering if they are about me. How much did they know that I didn't?

I ask, "Tell me exactly what the test says."

Mrs. Martin looks at me, then reads from the big folder filled with white and pink pages, "Your reading scores are at the level of a fifth grader."

I feel shame creep in. I'm shocked and exclaim, "What? I'm in eighth grade! Why didn't anyone tell me this before?"

Others around the table start speaking all at once. I notice I made them all uncomfortable, so I say, "All right let's put it in there, Mrs. Martin. I promise you that by the end of this year, we will take it out." She smiles at me. The meeting ends and we all walk out together to the main lobby. The school is empty with school letting out long ago.

Everyone goes out the lobby and I pretend to head out the side doors to go home. Instead I hurry across the lobby to the stairs and head back up to Mrs. Martin's room on the second floor inside the library.

I walk to Mrs. Martin's room and feel lucky that the door is open, I keep the light off. Inside I open the filing cabinet and take my big folder out. Shoving the file in my backpack, I sneak out of school unseen and head home. I stay up all night reading everything about me from kindergarten to eighth grade.

I make notes on paper to myself: vocabulary, reading comprehension, writing conventions and more. This is the night I decide I want to be smart.

At a party that weekend, I befriend a high school punk-Goth girl named Jonesy who turns me on to reading Mikhail Lermontov, Leo Tolstoy, Boris Pasternak, Karl Marx and Frederick Engels. First off, I don't understand anything I am reading, so I go out and buy two dictionaries. One is a pocket dictionary that I keep in my back pocket for the purpose of learning two words a day, until I know all of them. The other much bigger dictionary I keep by my side as I read, underlining every word I do not know and looking them up later. As my vocabulary develops, I become an even more voracious reader with an interest in an assortment of authors. I fall in love with Edgar Allen Poe, J.D. Salinger, Joseph Conrad, Herman Hesse, even stumbling on and over Sir James Frazier's *Golden Bough*. Many times, I don't understand a thing I am reading. But I love it. I sleep very little and stay up all hours of the night reading.

Then I start writing everyday – short poems, epic poems, short stories, even a book. At my prodding, my mother goes out and buys a display typewriter and sets it up in the basement on a wood desk with an old metal kitchen chair. I write my first novel, a complicated love story between two American teenagers living abroad. The characters are loosely based on a blend of Yuri Zhivago and Lara Antipova together with Kevin Arnold and Winnie Cooper. After careful research looking over books, maps, photographs, and microfiche archives at the library, I choose Valle d'Aosta as the backdrop for the story because it's located in northern Italy, bordering Switzerland to the north and France to the west. That way, the young couple can travel and have magnificently scenic adventures.

Every day I write and expand on the book. I share some of the chapters with Nanny, the only person I will share my writing with. Nanny loves love stories and persuades me to write more and more because she wants to know what will happen next. Every now and then I take some of my other writing to school to show Mrs. Martin. But never my book. Only Nanny sees the book.

By year end, Mrs. Martin and I anxiously await the post-school year test to show what I have learned. When Mrs. Martin shares the scores with me she is so proud. My vocabulary is now post-high school and reading and writing skills are off the charts. My grades in English and social studies are exceptionally high with nothing below ninety-eight percent. In my other subjects, I am average.

FIFTEEN

Surviving Against the Forces of Darkness – Exhibit A

I want to extend the metaphor Joe Tobin used earlier to describe his ambitions for me to overcome the Dark forces. The forces of Darkness embodies Althusserian conceptions of repressive and ideological state apparatuses, sustaining the conditions that (re)produce oppression against children with deafness. If I've been in training, as Joe suggested, during my formative years, this is where I (in the cosmology of Star Wars) decide to accept the challenge of fighting the Dark forces. Forces of ideological state apparatuses came to life through the special education process, one of its tentacles being the IEP meeting, scripted by ideological state apparatuses whose worldview could only see me as an always already failing mainstream deaf student. Why did I live under a cloud of thinking I was "special"? Why was I the last to know I wasn't doing well? I was doing well enough, for a mainstreamed student, if one thinks a fifth-grade vocabulary in eighth grade is good enough. What hurt me so much from that meeting was that I wanted the chance to be smart, and not be just mediocre.

Rachelle Hole's (2004) dissertation on narrative identities of three deaf women's life stories growing up in a hearing-dominated world uses post-structural analyses to uncover four discourses at work, including normalcy, difference, passing, and Deaf cultural discourses. Hole (2004) learns through the course of this study that cultural forces move the construction of identities into binaries (e.g., deaf/Deaf, d/Deaf/hearing, normal/abnormal, etc.). This has the effect of creating, as she terms it, unstable and shifting identities that directly link to phonocentric cultural climates that privilege one form of identity over the "other."

These cultural forces of Darkness work in mysterious ways. In order to uncover the mystification of special education networks, Bowker and Star (2002) recommend using a toolkit they call "infrastructural inversion" to get at how infrastructures enforce unquestioned practices and lifeworlds that stealthily empower the majority and impose on the marginalized. Bowker and Star explain "Infrastructural inversion means recognizing the depths of interdependence of technical networks and standards, on the one hand, and the real work of politics and knowledge production on the other" (2002, p. 34). This toolkit gives a snapshot of how special education categorization and sorting works to oppress deaf children. For the purpose of analyzing the preceding (where I accept the normalizing process) and subsequent (where I resist) vignettes, I want to draw with theoretical license from the infrastructural inversion toolkit and Althusser's notions of repressive and ideological state apparatuses as a frame of analysis to tease out how phonocentric/ableist cultural climates were surreptitiously at work during these two most memorable IEP meetings. The purpose of focusing on two instances, one where I accept and the other where I resist audism/ableism, is to give a more complete picture of these meetings across time and context.

The two tools I will borrow from the infrastructural inversion toolkit include: (1) "ubiquity," described as phenomena and artifacts that are embedded yet transparent, to uncover the insidious classification schemas that are dependent on cultural climates (e.g., normative and binary discourses; legal, medical, educational documents/forms/naming); and (2) "materiality and texture," meaning phenomena and artifacts that are learned as part of membership, link with conventions of practice, and are the embodiment of standards, exposing the material and symbolic artifacts of classifications and standards (e.g., special education and disability rights legislation; codification of disabilities; special education documentation).

For instance, audist cultural climates have the effect of masking ubiquitous special education normative classifications and standards. These normative systems set up binary markers privileging majoritarian constructions of abled/disabled, general/special education, or hearing/deaf (as I discussed earlier in terms of Foucault). The tool of ubiquity extends on conceptions of binaries by unmasking ways its subtle everyday framing drives how we think about and run our special education programs and IEP meetings. These binary markers are present in the ways that special education inhabits physical space. Think back to John's earlier comment "Oh, my God, he's not normal, send him down the BOCES hallway," or Mrs. Martin's room off of the library area. These spaces are created as a way to compartmentalize children with special needs for the purpose of sorting and classifying. The stigmas attached to these spaces have enormous implications for children navigating the mainstream scene. I remember many times throughout my school years waiting for children in the hallway to go away before entering these rooms. I did not want anyone to know, though they already did. There are those that are normal, and those that are not. I was not.

Special education assigns and uses legal and medical terms that make students normative subjects. Interactions with the special education professionals are examples of traditional unequal power dynamics as the experts work with the student or parents, each are performing expected roles that are culturally informed. An example of unequal power dynamics from the preceding vignette is when I ceded to their demands because the committee knew best. I thought. If I knew what I know now, I would have articulated that their preconceived notions of what I'm capable of are being vastly underestimated. These classifications, both (in)tangible, force special education students into the cycle of self-improvement that sees no end. Perfection can never be achieved because the ideal (becoming completely "hearing") is impossible. Audist/ableist special education discourses and their apparatuses serve to perpetuate the cycle of dependence on so-called experts and scientivistic ways of thinking to police and normalize children with deafness and disabilities into a hearing-dominated world.

Judith Butler (1999) tells us that our culture constructs regulative and normative discourses and artifacts. The classification discourses (e.g., special education student; deaf) and standardized artifacts (e.g., IEP goals) of special education are materially and symbolically represented in my IEP meeting. What materializes from this meeting is my continuing status as a special education student. Butler's ideas of cultural constructions of regulative and normative artifacts brings into full view the materiality of the classification and codification systems, both institutional and symbolic, that oppress d/Deaf children. This is one of the forms of masked epistemic violence that leads to linguicide and ethnocide of the d/Deaf community, as well as the *deafing* (silencing) and *dumbing* (disempowering) of children with deafness through the processes of mainstream special education.

I think in the case of this IEP meeting, special education served as a part of this extensive network to regulate and normalize me. While being codified as disabled/deaf, I was also being regulated and normalized to conform to the expectations of what special educators envisioned me to be — a mainstreamed special education student. The discourse in the vignette that I still remember so vividly demonstrates how the committee convinced me that I need to be a part of this system that works to remind me of my always already failing ears. I did not yet question the validity of these binaries or classifications.

Oftentimes, I tell people I'm a product of special education. When I say this, I'm thinking about how special education is not only an organizing unit for working with children with special needs, but also an end place where no one really escapes, continuing the cycle of dependency that feeds the forces of Darkness. Althusser (1972) explains that the end products of the "production of the conditions of production are reproduction" (p. 101). In this sense, by not involving me as a schoolchild in my education, I was not empowered but under "subjection to the ruling ideology" that viewed me as a nonparticipating special education subject, at least not with any authentic intent (Althusser, 1972, p. 104).

I didn't know it then, but I was coming to understand how it felt to be "othered" in uncovering the topography of normalizing forces during that IEP meeting; before then I never knew consciously how these forces ruled my life, my construction of who I was and wanted to be. I wanted to be smart according to these normalizing discourses I found myself immersed in during the meeting. I didn't know how until I read my files. It was easy to come up with a plan once I knew where to start. The people in the IEP meeting wanted to move me along at some predetermined pace; I wanted to get there faster. I thought once I achieved this, I would be done trying to overcome these normalizing forces, but I was wrong. The forces of Darkness are not so easily defeated. The empire always strikes back.

The repressive state apparatuses oppressing deaf children begin hierarchically with deficit-rehabilitative national government policies and legislation that moves into state and local communities and into our schools, classrooms, and IEP meetings. As these national courses of action are developed, Bowker and Star (2002) remind us that "Whatever appears as universal or indeed standard, is the result of negotiations, organizational processes, and conflict" (p. 44). Audist policymakers and stakeholders control the systems and people who work special education, while audist discourses dominate the minds of those who work with d/Deaf children and their families.

Many things shocked me from that day. I remember feeling hurt to learn everyone in that meeting already had preconceived notions of what I was capable of achieving and becoming. It hurt to have to start from such a deficit, to realize that I was not doing as well as I had been led to believe, nor was I told how far behind I was (without me having to ask repeatedly in this meeting). What would have happened if my mother had gone, or if Mrs. Martin had not asked me to come in my mother's place? I can't help but wonder where would I be today?

When I ask my mother she says, "Joey, I think you'd still be where you are today...successful. Maybe you would've just decided the same thing later; you always had this drive, so I do think you'd be where you are today."

I'm not so confident, "What if I did just let them make decisions for me? I think I would just have given up, and not had any real focus or idea how to get there. Those IEP papers gave me a goal, something to reach for; otherwise, I think I would have just kept on not knowing that I was so far behind."

"I always," my mother begins before I finish, "told you that you'd go to college since you were little, so you would've been successful."

My brother, me, and my sister, in that order, are the first in our family to go to college, so for our mom success is and always has been to get the college degree. Whatever else we decided to do was up to us, mostly (me wanting to be a pilot was sidelined early on). She continues, "You're the first in our family to get a doctorate, and I told you since you were a kid you'd be a doctor."

I start to smile because I know what she's going to say next.

"I went to how many psychics? And they all told me you'd be a doctor, even just after you were born...I thought you'd be a medical doctor, but you are a doctor...sorry, you will be a doctor...I don't want to jinx you," my mother teases me.

"Mom, you know I hate hospitals, so being a doctor was never an option," I say.

"I know, you not only had to deal with your hearing, but the cancer scare and all those operations," I can sense her feeling guilty, reminding me, "I was with you every minute, Joey," she's not just talking about the visits for my ears but my biopsies, multiple skin grafting operations, and the long arduous follow up path to make sure I was cancer free.

When my mother brings up "the cancer scare", I purposefully steer the conversation away with a simple, "Let's not go there, Mom."

She just says, "Oh, okay. I understand. That topic's off limits."

My mother and I move the conversation on to recent family news.

While talking with my mother, I think back to a conversation I had with Dr. Beth Blue Swadener while visiting a mutual friend in the hospital earlier that week.

I kept getting up and moving around, acting fidgety and Beth seemed to notice so she asked me, "How do you feel about hospitals, Joe?"

"They make me nervous," I say.

"I can see how this could be hard for you." Beth's nurturing side is what makes me admire her so much. I always feel like I can open up to her so easily. She always listens for how I feel.

"Yes, I spent a lot of time in hospitals growing up. For my ears, yes, but also for major skin grafting surgeries to prevent possible skin cancer. I was in the hospital for so many times."

Beth's face shows concern, "This must be difficult for you to come here, Joe, it took a lot strength for you to do that. Our body memories can have scars."

"Yes," I say, feeling like she understands why I'm so restless, I think of something I can do, "let me see if the nurses want this extra chocolate that no one wants." I get up a few more times to ask if the nurses need anything like coffee or soda. This is my routine when I go to hospitals. I can't stay in one place.

Quickly I tune back into what my mother was saying, and she turns the subject back around somewhat, hitting on exactly what I was thinking about, "You always loved visiting me at the hospital, when I worked the late shift, bringing me and all the other nurses coffee late at night…probably to see all the pretty nurses, yes?"

I chuckle, "No, Mom, they were all twice my age. I could only go to the hospital because you were there. I still can't go to hospitals now without feeling so much anxiety, I guess like many other people, too." I start to feel overwhelmed by the memories of those times in the hospital, so I steer the conversation back to my original question.

My mother understands I want to change topics, but she wants to make one thing clear before moving on, "Joey, you are a survivor."

Now I begin to wonder how these experiences also inform what I think of the medical and rehabilitative community, special education, and navigating the physical and emotional memories of the past. These forces of Darkness are a part of me and my past, and these forces are still at work today in the way I define myself, live my life, and conduct this research project.

I ask John the same question I asked my mother: Where would I be today if I didn't stand up in this or any other meeting?

John immediately reaches for familiar words in our family "You're a survivor; you are also tough to have hung in there. When everyone thinks you're going to fail, you take that as a dare."

Right away my mind starts to drift off to a memory from being in class with Joe Tobin. We were having a class talk about the idea of "always already failing" brought up in a discussion of Julie Kaomea's postcolonial work on indigenous Hawaiian children in school. I remember someone in class saying that what "always already failing" means is that we are all fighting against these forces that seek to privilege one way of doing and knowing over another. For those that are "othered," we will always fail because preconceived notions will always precede the person.

I remember feeling so miserable by this thought in the context of my own life. It felt so disempowering. I half-heartedly retorted, "Then this means there's no reason to fight back. That means we are all always already failing."

"Isn't there some comfort in knowing that we are *all* always already failing?" Joe asks me.

"Well, I guess if that means I don't have to feel like I need to meet these expectations that I never will meet, I guess, that is good," I say, though still somewhat unsure how this way of thinking would reconcile with my own life story. Now after going through this journey, I think I do know for sure that this *is* good. Only I can release myself from this phonocentric prison.

SIXTEEN

Captain of the Safety Patrol Team and the Flux Capacitor

Mr. Bradley, my fifth-grade teacher, is a tall man with thick-rim black glasses and a balding head. He pushes himself away from his desk and stands to speak:

I will now...

My hearing aid's battery dies. I think: Oh, crap.

I open up my desk to pull out a new battery. I replace the old battery with a new one. The hearing aid starts to squeak real loud. I realize I must be making a lot of noise because Mr. Bradley has stopped speaking. He stands in front of the room tapping his foot real fast, waiting on me.

I look up from my desk and see everybody is looking at me, some classmates give me a mean look and others just looked annoyed with me. I watch the prettiest girl in our class, Kristy, whisper something to Little Johnny. Quickly I put my squealing hearing aid back on and Mr. Bradley, clears his throat to start again:

I will now announce the winners!

Everybody gets all excited again. The room is silent. I watch a few classmates put their arms out over their desks with their fingers crossed. Others close their eyes. While the rest just look up at Mr. Bradley like he is Pat Sajak on *Wheel of Fortune*.

Mr. Bradley plays the role of game show host, he goes over the rules again: members of the team are selected by vote from each teacher in the Sylvan Avenue Elementary School.

The prize: Being a member of the Safety Patrol Team.

Mr. Bradley nods in the direction of Kristy, who plays Vanna White, she goes to the closet, pulls out a box labeled in bold letters "Safety Patrol" and places it on Mr. Bradley's big desk. Kristy then sits back down in her seat. Mr. Bradley walks to the front of the class and looks into the box a bit.

I sit there in my seat with my legs shaking nervously. I just can't wait. I cross my fingers and try to cross my toes in my sneakers too. I spent the last week lobbying hard with former teachers from kindergarten and on up to vote for me.

Mr. Bradley explained about all this in the meeting last week. Safety Patrol Team members enforce school rules: no running, no gum, no wandering the halls while classes are on, or wandering the halls before or after school. Each team member gets to wear the orange reflector safety patrol belt and a silver metal badge. Safety patrol officers also get the carbon copy Ticket Pad. The Pink sheet goes to the student; Yellow goes to Main Office; Blue goes to Safety Patrol Team filing cabinet. The Safety Patrol Team has the power to write any student a ticket. Three tickets gets you a meeting with Mr. Weik, the principal.

Mr. Bradley stands up tall, straightens his tie and announces the Safety Patrol Team members for the upcoming school year: Garret, Sean, Freckles, Little Johnny, and Kristy.

I wait. I look around, all five of them stand up and go to the front of the classroom to collect their orange belts, badges, and ticket pads. I'm shocked.

I think to myself: How is this possible? This is horrible. Absolutely horrible. I feel all my energy just empty out of me. I feel so let down.

Mr. Bradley tells the class to give the new Safety Patrol Team a round of applause, makes a quick joke about everybody better be extra nice to the team members now that they can give tickets, and tells everybody to take their social studies textbooks out.

When Sean passes me, I give him the headshake — which is a slow downward nod while making eye contact — to let him know I'm happy for him. He gives the headshake back. Freckles just looks over to me some. We don't talk in school, only around the neighborhood. That's her rule, not mine. Freckles doesn't want anyone at school to know we hang out because her friends all hate me, especially Kristy.

I'm not shocked that Garret got it because he is the class genius. Everybody has a crush on Kristy, even the teachers, so I'm not surprised she got it too. But Little Johnny? That does shock me. He's always in Mr. Weik's office. I guess he will be the enforcer. Someone has to bully us since Commander moved to Middle School now.

Everybody takes out their social studies textbook and Mr. Bradley says, Oh, I almost forgot.

Everybody stops rummaging through their desk for their textbooks and looks up. Collectively we're all hoping he'll say he forgot we have a special — gym, art, or library or something. But he doesn't. Instead he says, I forgot to tell you who will be the leading officers of the Safety Patrol Team — can't have a team without a Captain. Let me get that sheet out again, hang on...

I can see Sean, Freckles, Kristy, Garrett, and Little Johnny getting all excited.

Mr. Bradley finds the sheet, Ah, here it is. Officers are: Captain...Joey...hu?

He looks down at the sheet and says, Oh, my. How did I miss this? Sorry, Joey, you too are a member of the Safety Patrol Team. I don't know why you weren't on the other list. Doesn't make sense.

Mr. Bradley rummages around his desk looking for something. Confused. I don't really care because he just said it. I'm a member of the Safety Patrol Team! He can't take it back now. Not after telling the whole class.

OK, he says, getting himself back together, Everybody listen up, change here: Captain is Joey, Lieutenants are Freckles and Kristy, Sergeant is Sean, Garret is the Treasurer and Little Johnny will be Crossing Guard Assistant with Patrol Officer Petski.

I hear Little John let out, Ah, G'damn, I can't stand Officer Pear-ski.

Some kids chuckle at Little Johnny's comment. Officer Petski is known as Officer Pear-ski because her body looks like a pear. Only very few kids dare say that to her face. She is a real police officer so one time, I heard from Freckles who heard from her old sister, Frances, that Officer Petski arrested a kid for calling her a "pear" and she handcuffed him, put him in the police car and took him to jail. No one has heard from the kid since.

Mr. Bradley ignores Little Johnny's outburst and says, Round of applause everyone for the Safety Patrol Team.

He continues after everyone is done clapping, Okay, okay, great, thanks everybody. Safety Patrol Team, look up here, lunch time we meet to discuss what needs to be done to get started today, Okay?

All of us nod.

Everybody claps again. Mr. Bradley grabs the remaining orange Safety Patrol Belt and hands it to me, then picks up the badge with his right hand and the ticket pad with his left to pass to me. I see the silver badge with a blue middle and the words: Captain.

I'm so excited.

I look over to Sean, Alright! I make a fist and pound the air with it.

Sean gives me a high-five and says, Cool, now we get to be together.

Freckles breaks her rule: she comes over and gives me a pat on the shoulder on her way to sharpen her pencil.

Kristy looks at me like I'm a star. Like she's impressed by me for the first time.

Little Johnny seems pissed. He keeps repeating to himself, Officer Pear-ski, ugh, Pearski, ugh. I hate her.

Mr. Bradley doesn't have patience when it comes to falling behind on our work so he says, Alrighty there, let's get back to work. Social studies text, page sixty-four, which is chapter 8, you need to read this and answer the questions at the end of the chapter. Any questions?

Two kids ask to go to the bathroom and he tells them to grab the pass and hurry up to get back here.

They don't run but they walk fast out of the classroom.

I'm so excited, I keep looking at my badge and belt and pad. I love it.

Mr. Bradley walks up to my desk, says, Congratulations, Joey. Make us proud, Okay?

I will, I say.

Okay, he says, now put all that Safety Patrol stuff away in the coat closet. When it's about fifteen minutes before school lets out, you will remind me to let you and the team go downstairs to get ready – you know, the cones, ropes, and stuff get set up, see if Officer Petski needs anything, then get your team in position before the bell lets out. Sounds okay? You ready for this big responsibility?

He grins at me. I think he is enjoying how serious I'm taking all this. I ain't goofing around on this one.

Mr. Bradley reminds me, Go, go get that stuff into the closet and get to work on that chapter.

I say, Yes, Mr. Bradley. Thank you, Mr. Bradley.

He turns around and kneels down to talk with Little Johnny who seems really pissed off about having to work with Officer Petski as her crossing guard assistant. Mr. Bradley stays kneeling and whispering to Little Johnny for a good amount of time.

I get back to my desk and try to get to work on reading the chapter. But I have to stop and start over several times because I'm thinking about being the Captain of the Safety Patrol Team. I'm going to be wearing the Captain badge. I get to tell people what to do. I'm important.

A lot of time goes by, and I can see that my classmates are now finishing answering the chapter questions. Some of them start to get up to turn in their answers to Mr. Bradley. It's close to lunch so I know we don't have much time left. I start to panic I will fall behind and not be able to go to the Safety Patrol Team meeting at lunch. So I look over to Garret sitting in his chair next to me. He is almost done with all his questions but he is struggling with his pencil for some reason. Garrett gets up to go sharpen it over by Mr. Bradley's desk.

I look over at Garret's sheet to see what he wrote down for his answers. Mr. Bradley is distracted so I take a good look down to see what the answers are. I write them down on my sheet too. Changing a few words here and there to make it look a little different. I'm almost done when Garret finishes with his pencil sharpening and I have to look away. He sits down. Nobody noticed. I feel so relieved I only have to answer the last question and I'm done.

Mr. Bradley says to the class, Okay, okay, everybody, stop, put down your pencils. You can finish these up when we get back from lunch. Let's go lineup for lunch now. First row, go.

I look at Sean just ahead of me and a row over. We're both going to grab lunch together and stand next to one another on the lunch line.

Second row, go.

The volume in the classroom increases with excited voices. Lunch and recess are here so everyone is trying to talk to everyone at the same time.

Mr. Bradley speaks over all of us, Okay, okay, Safety Patrol Team: Get your hot lunches and bring them back here for the meeting, okay?

Row three and four, let's go, he yells, Row five and six next. Move it, let's go.

I get up and move to the front of the class where the line has formed. Sean comes over to me. We stand next to each other in line and shuffle along together as we go down the hallway with Mr. Bradley leading us until we get to the cafeteria lady who makes us go on another line.

We get our lunches and come back to the classroom where Mr. Bradley is already eating his cafeteria lunch.

I ask him, How did you get lunch so fast?

He says, Well, teachers have their own lunch room.

Oh, I say, That must be cool.

You think? He asks.

I look at Sean, then back to Mr. Bradley, Yea, I do think that is so cool. Do you have the same food?

Yes, pretty much. But we have a Coke and candy machine in there too.

Sean and I are so surprised. I ask, Can we use it now that we are on the Safety Patrol Team?

Mr. Bradley laughs. Haha, he goes, heehee, haha. It gets to be a bit weird because he keeps laughing. Sean looks at me like don't make him laugh like that again. I give him the look back like I know, I know.

Mr. Bradley stops laughing, looks up at me, says, That's a good question, Joey. Let me go find out about that and get back to you.

I say, Okay.

Sean sits down at his desk a few seats back but Mr. Bradley says, No, No, Sean. Make a circle with the desks so we can all sit together and talk and eat our lunch. Me and Sean move the desks into a circle. Garrett, Little Johnny, Kristy, and Freckles come into the room. We all sit down and go over the plan for today. I'm so excited. My job is to make sure everybody is doing their job. I get to be the leader.

When the meeting is over, we get to hang out in the classroom with Mr. Bradley until lunch is over. We all play Connect Four. I ask Mr. Bradley, Can I go to the bathroom?

He looks at me and asks, I don't know. Can you?

I laugh. He always does this routine. I ask again, May I go to the bathroom?

Yes, you may, he says.

Little Johnny asks too, Mr. Bradley, I need to go too – may I?

Yes, you both may go, he says.

We grab the wooden bathroom passes that are just a piece of blue painted 2 x 4 with Mr. Bradley's name printed on each side.

I walk down the hallway with Little Johnny next to me. He keeps looking down at his feet. I keep looking at him to gauge what he's thinking. I know he was mad before that he got stuck being a crossing guard assistant for Mrs. Petski. I wonder if he is still pissed?

Hey, Little Johnny, I say, Hey, are you piss'd?

He looks at me, Says, Shut up, Deaf kid. Just coz yu da Capt'n don't mean nothing. I dun't got'a listn' tu yu. Got it?

Little Johnny pokes me in the chest in front of the bathroom door. I'm scared to go into the bathroom with him because then no one can see us. Little Johnny may be little but he loves to fight dirty; he bites; he kicks and punches in the groin; he scratches and claws; he even picks up weapons to beat people with. Everybody knows if you fight Little Johnny, you better be ready to fight dirty.

All this doesn't matter because he pulls me by my shirt into the bathroom. Little Johnny looks like he's going to go Commander on my ass. Only this time, Commander is not even here.

He holds my shirt, Yu think yur special coz yu Capt'n, 'ey?

I don't say anything. I'm scared to fight and get hurt. I don't want to lose my job as the Captain of the Safety Patrol Team too. Surely the Captain can't be fighting, I think to myself. I'm not sure what to do. Do I punch in self-defense when he hits me or do I just let him hit me? Or do I try to run out of the bathroom before he gets me and run for help down the hallway?

I don't think I'll make it to the door, if I try to run. He's already got a hold of me so I know I won't make it far. He'll just punch me in the head from behind.

Hey Deaf kid! Stop looking away from me! Look at me, he screams into my ear. I can see the veins in his face and throat. I can see the rage, the anger he has for me. He hates me.

I can feel some pee trickle a bit down my leg. I look at the toilets and urinals nearby. I wish so badly I could just use one real quick. I wish I could ask for a time-out like we do in street ball when a car is approaching.

De---af! K----id!

De---af! K---id!

Spit sprays into my face. He screams into my ear. I wonder if Mr. Spanky, the art teacher everybody brings birthday cupcakes to for a birthday spank countdown, will hear us. Mr. Spanky's classroom is right next door. For some odd reason, I feel faint. Oh, I think to myself, please, please pass out, please faint. I beg for some powerful force to just make me faint, that way Little Johnny will only have a sack of potatoes in his hand.

De---af kid!

De---af kid!

I can't stop looking at the veins on his forehead, in his face, neck, shoulders, arms. He spits on me again, yells:

Answer me, now, or I'll punch yu in the face. Answer me!

Yu think yur special coz yu Capt'n, 'ey?

I know I have to answer him this time. His left fist is cocked six inches from my face, ready to unload. My knees give a little. I let out my answer and a cry at the same time:

No!

What yu say?

I repeat, No! Tears stream down my face, fall off my chin. I can't hold the pee, it comes. First it wets my pants entirely. Then it pours out all over the floor. Little Johnny takes a minute to realize what happened. He is slow to respond.

The pee drenches my pants and makes a large puddle around us. Little Johnny is standing in my pee. The soles of his sneakers are starting to soak and stink like my urine. I can see the white of his sneakers stain the yellow of my pee.

Little Johnny has a look of absolute horror on his face. He holds the back of my head, holds my hair tighter. But suddenly I feel him let go. He jumps out of the pee puddle and lands outside of it on the dry floor. He yells, What the hell?!

Little Johnny looks shocked.

I'm not. I'm used to this. I already know what I have to do. Go to the Nurse Nancy's office and she has a change of clothes for me. She'll let me clean myself off in the big bathroom she has down there. It has bars on the side of each wall for when you are in a wheelchair.

I don't say anything to Little Johnny. He just keeps tiptoeing around the bathroom floor where it is dry and keeps repeating himself, What the hell? What the hell!

I get up from the puddle. This is my time-out I'd wished for.

My pants are soaked, my sneakers too. Even the bottom of my shirt has urine on it. I smell.

Little Johnny washes his hands and puts some soap on a paper towel and tries to wash away the urine splattered all over his sneakers. His white sneakers were yellow and now they become a mixture of the brown dye from the paper towels and soap starts to mesh into the fabric. He's just making it worse. I don't say anything. I just try to dry myself down with some paper towels so I can walk the hallway without making a mess with my pee.

I leave Little Johnny in the bathroom without saying a word to him. He doesn't try to say anything to me. So I go quietly.

I walk down the hallway a bit, make a right and go down the stairwell that leads out into the lobby, walk diagonally through the lobby past the main office, and take the right hallway down to the nurse's office halfway down.

I walk into the office and Nurse Nancy is helping some little kid with a band-aid. She looks up at me. Sees the pee all over my pants, shoes, and shirt. Nurse Nancy doesn't move away from the kid, she says, Go ahead to the bathroom, Joey. I'll go get your bag now.

I wait for her to bring me the brown paper bag that has a change of clothes, a shirt, socks, and some underwear. I hate dressing in the school bathroom. I don't like it because I'm always afraid some classmate will open the door, see me in my underwear, and use it to make fun of me. I still like to wear my superhero undies.

Nurse Nancy bangs on the door, says something. But I can't hear her because I can't see her lips.

I open it a bit, she hands me the brown paper bag and leaves. I take it and strip my clothes off. I'm naked in the school bathroom. It feels cold. I turn on the hot water at the sink, let it get warm. I put some soap on a paper towel and wash my body some. I try to find the places where the pee went. I scrub myself clean. Then I take a new paper towel and wet that but don't put soap on it. This I use to rinse myself.

When I'm done washing the pee off of me, I put my fresh clothes on. I'm excited Mom put my Superman undies in the bag because they are my favorite. I take the peed on clothes and put them in the brown bag to give to Nurse Nancy.

I realize after I put the clothes in the bag that I don't have any fresh shoes.

Ah crap, I say aloud.

Nurse Nancy hears me, she comes to the door, knocks, peeks her head around some. Can I come in?

I know she wants to come in so I say, Yes, come here.

When she opens the door I hand her the brown bag. She takes it. I say to her, I can't put my shoes on because they smell like pee.

Nurse Nancy says, Let me see. She picks them up, quickly realizes they are soaked, puts them back down on the floor, walks over to the sink and washes her hands. She says, Let me take care of those.

Nurse Nancy smiles. I know she's trying to be nice but it feels weird.

She looks at me, smiling, like none of this happened and asks, Do you want to talk?

Nah, I say.

I'm more worried about how I'm going to go back to class without sneakers. Everybody will know something happened, if they don't already know. Little Johnny may not want to tell anyone because he'll get into trouble.

Nurse Nancy looks at me, I already spoke with Mr. Bradley. He said to call him when you're ready to come back.

I can't go back, I say to her.

Why? She asks.

Because my sneakers, I don't have sneakers to wear. I can't wear those.

Nurse Nancy looks at me, like she's trying to think of something.

How about you go to Mrs. Kapell's? She's your favorite teacher, yes?

Okay, I say. I'm excited.

Nurse Nancy says, Hold on, sit down, I'll be right back. Mrs. Kapell's room is right next door so I'm guessing she is going to see if I can come over.

A few minutes go by. I sit there in the office. Nurse Nancy's office is white. Everything everywhere is white. Even the desk and chairs are white and the curtains around the beds are white. It looks like a hospital in a school.

Through the door into the office comes Mrs. Kapell. She has a worried look on her face and immediately gives me a hug.

Mrs. Kapell leans down, says, This must have been so hard for you. Are you okay?

I never understood how Mrs. Kapell always knew about how things feel before you even told her.

I'm okay, I say. Mrs. Kapell is not convinced, she gives me the look like she knows I'm holding back.

Nurse Nancy walks up next to Mrs. Kapell and says to me, Mrs. Kapell said you can stay with her until school ends today. Is that okay?

Yup, I say. I'm so happy.

Mrs. Kapell takes me to her room. She has stuff she needs to look at so she asks me what I want to do until she is done and we can play a game.

I say, I want to make something.

She asks me, What do you want to make?

I say, I want to make a flux capacitor!

Mrs. Kapell laughs some, Why?

Because then we can put it on your car and go back to the future! I'm so excited with my plan.

She laughs again, says, okay, so how you going to make one? What do you need?

I don't know, I say, Maybe a box.

How about a shoe box?

Yea, that'll work.

Mrs. Kapell gives me a shoebox. Inside of it are some batteries, duct tape, bolts and screws, and an assortment of odd items. I ask her, What's this for?

She laughs, Mr. Kapell and I were cleaning out one of our drawers at home and found some of this stuff to put in here. I brought it to school in the shoebox to try to find a place for this stuff here.

Oh, can I use it?

Sure, Mrs. Kapell says, Go ahead. You go build your flux cap –

– capacitor, I say, Flux capacitor.

Yes, she says, go build the flux capacitor and by then I should be done with my work and we can play any game you want.

Okay, I say. I get to work building my flux capacitor.

Mrs. Kapell goes and sits by her desk, she writes and reads stuff.

After a while, Mrs. Kapell comes over and asks, Do you want to play a game now?

I say, No.

Oh, Mrs. Kapell says, What do you want to do?

I want to build this flux capacitor.

Alright, then let's do that she says. Mrs. Kapell seems excited, she asks, What do we need to do to finish it? It looks pretty complicated, how does it work?

I explain to Mrs. Kapell how the batteries use energy to light up all the parts I've taped together in the box.

She says, That is so interesting. So how does all that make you go back in time?

I say, Well, I haven't been able to figure out the time machine parts yet. I'm going to need more time.

Mrs. Kapell says, Well, you can take it home and work on it some. Do you want to do that?

Yea, I say, Good idea.

The warning bell goes off and school is about to be let out. I ask Mrs. Kapell, What am I going to do without my sneakers? How do I walk home?

I'll take you, she says.

Great! I say. I'm so excited, I ask, Can we try out the flux capacitor on your car?

Of course, Mrs. Kapell says.

Cool!

SEVENTEEN

"Why take a chance?"

After my ninth grade year, an individualized education plan meeting is held at an old Cape-Cod-style house used by the school district for extra office space. I now go regularly to these meetings and actively participate. A few minutes before two o'clock, I drive to the meeting across town in the white 1987 two-door Mustang LX my mother passed from my older brother, John, then on down to me. My mother named the car Mustang Sally but everybody calls her Sally for short.

Sally is very popular. Because I was left back in kindergarten, I'm one of the oldest in my class and the first to get my driver's permit as a freshman in high school. Having Sally strengthens my stock in the popularity pecking order that exists in high school. Even a few juniors and seniors without cars befriend me, which in the complicated politics of adolescence equates to bonus points that can then be cashed in for access to the much cooler senior parties. My best friends, Sean and Dave, both freshmen too, love our newfound celebrity thanks to Sally.

I'm early for the IEP meeting, so I park in the small parking lot behind the school district building, sit there, and think about what it is that I want to say in this meeting. I spent all last night preparing.

I'm expecting resistance.

I interned with a lawyer's office this past school year as part of a social studies class assignment so I prepare for the IEP meeting as a lawyer would for a court case. This includes index cards after index cards of notes with specific talking points. I sit in the car with the windows down and try to visualize success and what victory will feel like if I can succeed at what it is I'm setting out to do this afternoon. The edgy energy makes me shake my knees and feet constantly. I'm nervous with anticipation, wanting to ask to be placed in the honors program for tenth grade.

For this special occasion I put in my hearing aid that I stopped wearing entirely earlier this year. I would not wear another one until my second year of college, feeling somehow that I want to prove to everyone that I don't need any help and can still be very successful. This becomes increasingly difficult as school becomes more challenging.

When I arrive inside the building, I'm excited to see my speech pathologist from elementary school, Joan Kapell is here to replace my absent high school speech therapist. I'm relieved I have the hearing aid on because she would have questioned me and given me a hard time about not wearing it. We chat some, but the meeting starts right away. The committee discusses my progress and how exceptional my grades are this year.

First I start out slowly thanking everyone for their support and pause before saying, "I feel like I'm ready to take honors English and social studies next year."

I look around the room, most faces don't look pleased and I move my eyes to Mrs. Kapell so I don't lose my strength. She smiles at me, nods encouragement.

Someone asks, "Why, Joe?"

"I want the challenge, and I find the classes I'm in go too slow. My grades are really good." I say with some defensiveness in my voice.

Initially no one moves or says anything. Everyone just looks around the table to see who will jump in first. It's obvious every one of them has something they want to say. Then in chorus, voices from all over the table shoot out at me. "We've never had a student receiving special education services take honors classes." "You are doing so well, so that's why you should stay in the regular classes, Joe." "Your grades are really good. Why take a chance?" "Do you really want the extra work?" "What do you have to gain by doing this?"

I'm feeling really defensive now. I look over to Mrs. Kapell and see her speaking low to a person next to her. I can't read her lips or face to see what she thinks or is saying. The person she spoke to looks at me and smiles. I think to myself: Is Mrs. Kapell politicking for me?

Someone finally suggests, "How about you start in the regular classes next year and if you are doing as well as you are now and still want to go into the honors classes, we can put you in there?"

I'm ready to spar verbally, "Good idea. How about instead we start me off in the honors classes next year and if I struggle then I can be pulled out?"

It goes quiet again. I look around the table at the faces. Mrs. Kapell looks like she is trying to hold back a knowing smile. She already knows how I can be.

Everyone else at the table has these contemplative looks on their faces. After some deliberation, someone says, "Sounds fair to me, Joe. But no grades below ninety or we will have to pull you." Another adds, "We will speak with your teachers to let them know about this agreement."

I'm feeling happy to get what I want, but still disappointed with their terms so I say, "Sure. A deal. I have a question, though: Do all honors students have to have a ninety or above to stay in the program?"

Some people smile at my parting question. No one answers. I'm surprised that a few of the committee members come up to me as we walk out and congratulate me. Mrs. Kapell gives me a big hug and a look like she's amused. I'm not sure if everyone is congratulating me for being in the honors program or for standing up for myself. I get in my car and as soon as I turn the corner, I take my hearing aid out, shoving it in my pocket.

EIGHTEEN

Surviving Against the Forces of Darkness – Exhibit B

Now back to the tools of ubiquity and materiality and using the Althusserian lens to expose how I resisted them in this IEP meeting. These instances where I accepted and resisted audism/ableism demonstrate the workings of IEP meetings as theatrical productions of classification, sorting, and interpellation. For example, when the anonymous committee member commented on not ever having had a mainstreamed special education student take honors classes, this person was speaking directly from the binary discourses that go unquestioned in our schools today about how to serve students with disabilities from a strengths perspective. Committee members were working under an audist/ableist worldview that had a stranglehold on special education and these IEP meetings, working as a mechanism to control and regulate the always already failing body.

There are multiple layers of ubiquitous binaries materialized in this vignette, including special education/gifted education, normal/abnormal, and hearing/deaf, echoing Rachelle Hole's (2004) findings about the multiplicity of identities – those chosen and assigned. Additionally there are the binaries of school officials interpreting the globalized legal mandates that compete or coexist with more localized contexts that may not even be known such as the desire to keep students enrolled in special education for resources even if they no longer need them, as it seems was true in my case. Another binary that materializes in the vignette is that of the anonymous committee member naming or identifying me as a "special education" student as opposed to a "mainstreamed" student, which would have been more accurate though nonetheless still a label. As a final point, the binary of expectations that I should maintain a ninety average or above, while my hearing peers did not. As Bowker and Star (2002) noted earlier, these are the infrastructures that served as (un)official barriers that are embedded in the processes (e.g., IEP meetings) of special education, even as they are seemingly so transparent with the use of standardized forms, legal mandates, and the inclusion of families. Judith Butler (1999) reminds us that these normative discourses and artifacts are constructed by our cultural climates. Butler's work also warns us to think about how these categorical dualities can be dangerous. She cautions that *being* a special education/gifted education student, *being* a normal/abnormal person, and a *being* hearing/deaf person are performances that are destined to fail. For instance, How does someone perfectly perform being able-bodied or disabled? Even the definitions of these terms are contested and constantly shifting and shaping. Butler would argue that these categories of special education/gifted education, normal/abnormal, hearing/deaf are too hard to pin down and too idyllic to achieve.

I was recently talking with a classmate at Arizona State University, Ashley Sullivan, about these infrastructures that were barriers for me and something came up in our conversation that I had buried deep in the recesses of my memory. Both of us grew up on Long Island, New York, where Regents diplomas are awarded to students that complete a rigorous predetermined curriculum that includes required coursework and high-stakes state-wide mandated testing. The alternative is to receive a "local diploma" that has lesser status, especially when applying to state universities.

Since both of us left Long Island many years ago, I ask Ashley, "Do you remember the Regents diploma?"

"Yes, why?" She asks.

"I never got a Regents diploma. I only got the local diploma. It made me so angry to find out just before graduation that I would not get it. Even worse, I was supposed to get an Honors Regents diploma because of the classes I was taking in the honors program."

"Why did that happen? It seems to still hurt you." I sense Ashley immediately understands the disappointment, she can sense my shame.

"It does still hurt. I was told by my counselor early in tenth grade that since I could not take Spanish or French to complete the foreign language requirement for a Regents diploma, instead I could take an additional load of fine arts classes and other electives. American Sign Language would not count to meet the language requirement, I was told. I decided to take the honors route so I could also get the coveted Honors Regents diploma. About three years later, just before graduation I learned that this coursework plan would not meet the requirements and I would as a substitute get the local diploma. I remember thinking this is just representative of my whole public school career."

Ashley asks, "It makes you feel hurt that you worked so hard for it?"

"Yes, and still even after following their rules, I still did not get it."

There are multiple examples of infrastructures that were barriers for me in my school life world. There are too many of these stories to tell, but each one, like the vignettes and the diploma memory, reveal the institutionalizing processes and policies of categorization and sorting schools enforce. These classification discourses and artifacts are ubiquitous in the way they reinforce/enforce normative classification and sorting systems. Not being able to take American Sign Language to count for the language requirement is a direct result of the ubiquitous binaries of what counts as a "real" language. It was simultaneously embedded and transparent. In the early 1990s when I was in high school, American Sign Language had still not been accepted as a "legitimate" language (by phonocentric standards) despite renowned sign language linguist, William Stokoe's research since the 1970s showing visual languages display as much complexity and beauty as spoken languages. The phonocentric cultural climate early on in the 1990s was embedded in the school's (or state's) decision to not see American Sign Language as equivalent to spoken languages. Likewise, the privileging of spoken over visual language was transparent. I remember complaining to school officials (at this point, I was very adept at advocating for myself) to no avail. The infrastructure could not be questioned, challenged, or resisted. So I took the local diploma on graduation day with bittersweet feelings.

As I'm writing about this, my mother calls me from New York to check in on me and say hello. I tell her that I'm writing about the IEP meeting and local diploma. She vaguely remembers, asking "What's the difference? You've already graduated from high school and college. It wasn't a barrier. They [the school] were wrong to do it. That counselor you had then was an idiot. But the other one – what was his name…"

"Mr. McDonough," I throw in.

"Yes, he was a good man. Remember he made you filet mignon at his house, and helped to plan your [admission] interview for Bates."

"He was a sweet man."

"The first one was the one that told you to not go to college. I didn't tell you, but I called the principal right after. No one…no one tells my children they're not going to college," my mother's tone gets very agitated.

"You called the principal?"

"Yes," she says.

I start to laugh, thinking about my mom. No one knows better how to stand their ground than her. She is the ultimate survivor. My mom is known in our family for personally having spoken with chief executive officers of *Fortune* 500 companies to complain about services and products. She goes straight to the top every time. Always telling us, if someone says no, then simply move on up the chain to whoever is in charge until you get what you want. I recognize that I'm privileged to have been able to grow up in this environment, especially considering the barriers that were/are placed in front of me as I navigate(d) the hearing-world.

"What did you say?" I'm still laughing, thinking about the poor principal who must have wished more than anything to get off the phone with my mother.

My mom laughs too, "I said what I always say. What I've been saying since the time I had to stand in front of the board of education with your speech therapist, Joan Kapell and argue that you had a right to go to public school. I told everyone in the room, 'Joey deserves the same chance as everyone else.'"

"That's all," I'm thinking something must be missing.

"That's all I said publicly," she goes quiet and I start to wonder what she is hiding.

"What do you mean publicly?" I'm curious, almost unsure if I should ask because my mom is known for going to great lengths to get what she wants.

"That's basically what I said to everyone at the board of education meeting. Joan argued on your behalf, telling them that you showed how brilliant a child you were with such a profound loss, to read lips so well. She told them that you taught yourself how to read lips from the time you were born and on. We didn't even realize how much of a loss you had until just before kindergarten, and even then we weren't sure. You read lips so well that no one knew your loss was so much."

I realize she didn't answer the question, "Mom, what did you say to the board privately."

"Not much," she says, "the superintendent and I did have a talk," my mom's voice sounds mischievous and she continues, "I killed him with kindness."

I grasp she is not going to tell me this because I'm planning to write about it, so I let it go for now and move the direction of the conversation to the agreement with the IEP team that I would maintain a ninety average and above (I will not tell my mother, even to this day, that I did not wear those hearing aids when not at home).

I ask my mom, "Why did it always have to be so much of a production to get the school to agree on giving me a chance so many times?"

"People can only do what they know to do," she says. At first, I take this as one of my mom's vague statements meaning the conversation about memories is over so we can move on to current family news, but then I think about this some more, and throw one last question at her.

"So you're saying that people at the school – not all – but most placed these barriers in front of me because it is all they know how to do?"

"No," she says, "what they know to do – what they already think they should do."

I've learned over the years not to tell my family or friends that I'm impressed with their insights, especially when I see a connection to theory I've studied, because it seems patronizing. I don't mean it that way. I'm impressed when theory comes to life as in my mom's thoughts being so reflective of the always already-ness and the connections between power and knowledge that exists in the world, even though she has never read about these philosophical terms and ideas. It seems to confirm the universality of these ways of thinking.

I go back to her comment, "You're saying that they already had their thoughts, so their preconceived notions of what I was or could do are what drove their thinking?"

"Yes, but you are forgetting that they *had* to do some of the things they did," she says.

I'm unsure what she means, "Why did they *have* to place barriers in front of me?"

"Because they saw you as deaf. I showed them how to see you as Joey," she says.

Thoughts flash across my mind as she tells me this. I think about the ubiquitous binaries (e.g., deaf/hearing, able/disabled, special/general education student) showing their material selves through these barriers. I also think back to the Joe Tobin's class discussion on "always already failing," back to his question if it is a comfort to know that we are all "always already failing." This leads us to the metaphysical question of agency that I will address in detail later, whether we control our fate or does the conditions we live in control how we think and live our lives (or somewhere along this continuum). Althusser (1972) tell us these conditions of reproduction materialize themselves in many ways, both subtle and transparent; social formation influences our ideology of understanding and living in the world. Schools serve as sites of social formation and enculturation. Ideology is everywhere; it is embedded in our thoughts and our institutions.

Being a "product of special education," having grown up being a part of the special education establishment, has given me insights into the workings of repressive and ideological state apparatuses that seek to normalize and regulate me (as well as deaf children in schools today). Today the battles in our schools are both much different and also much the same. Children with deafness are being mainstreamed with more frequency today than when I was a child. The schools themselves are changing.

Schools for the deaf are closing at astronomical rates (though a few have been reopened or new ones created as a reaction to these closures) because of the mainstreaming phenomena that gained steam in the 1980s, and the inclusion discourses of the Americans with Disabilities Act, and legislative mandates for equal access for special education students in the 1990s. The landscape has changed but the forces of Darkness still prevail. The process of passing on Deaf culture and sign is a peer-to-peer enculturation practice that is fast losing ground due to the mainstream movement and to cochlear implants. Deaf clubs have moved away from the brick and mortar meetings of the past to online communities (again, there is a revival of these clubs in some cities such as Deaf Coffee Chat in Phoenix run by Donna Leff, a professor of ASL at Arizona State University).

Phonocentric ideologies present in my IEP meeting show how the repressive state apparatuses of government and education policies and legislation of the time came to fruition during my time in school. These institutions reinforced/enforced deficit perspectives with constructions of normalcy that privilege majoritarian society, while "othering" those that show difference. I don't have access to my IEP paperwork anymore (though I have made repeated requests to gain access to these files from the school district and I have not been able to get a response), so I can't deconstruct this artifact word by word to frame how these documents impacted my own life in school while growing up. I only have my memories and those of my informants to help me along the way.

Wendy Luttrell (2005) suggests that in life-story analysis "We listen and make sense of what we hear according to particular theoretical, ontological, personal and cultural frameworks" (p. 243). As researchers, Luttrell (2005) continues, "there is always the worry that the voices and perspectives of those we study will be lost or subsumed to our own views and interests" (p. 243). While merging counter-storytelling tactics with multiple frames of analyses to examine the collective memory of my family, friends, and mentors, I have tried to show the tensions, contradictions, and plot points along the story of my life that make me who I am today.

NINETEEN

"Valedictorian of the retards"

On graduation day for high school, I'm so excited sitting in the crowd with my best friends, Sean and Dave, near me. We're preparing to launch a few forbidden beach balls, reaching as nondescriptly as possible to fill them up with air and then hide them under our gowns to avoid the hawking school staff looking for seniors ready to pull antics exactly like ours. They already failed. Looking around the school lawn where the ceremony is taking place, almost an acre of trees are smothered with white toilet paper, as if a Charmin monsoon passed through the night before. It was the three of us and a cadre of other pranksters in arms who stormed through at two in the morning, after a night of illicit and unbridled celebration. This was our ill-conceived, adolescent way of saying good-bye to all we'd ever known. We were college bound.

After the ceremony, I'm standing under a tree for shade, and one of the teachers from my high school comes up to me. I'm thinking he's going to congratulate me, wish me well.

"Hi, Joe." He looks me over in my gown, grinning to himself for some reason.

"Hey, Mr. Zornik,"[1] I counter.

"So, you're going to Bates College, huh?" We're about the same height, so I'm looking straight ahead to read his lips, ignoring the noise around us.

I smile with pride, "Yes."

Mr. Zornik shifts to leaning more on one foot, looks at me, eyes in a mock frown, "You were always the smartest of the retards. I can't believe that such a good school like Bates would accept a deaf kid like you," he jokingly punches me in the arm to put the exclamation on his comment, as if it were half a statement of fact as well as a joke, "tell them at Bates you were the valedictorian of the retards, they'll be impressed."

I walk away without saying anything to Mr. Zornik. If I did say anything I would not be able to keep myself from making a scene. I just want to go. I look for my family to go home. My mom is throwing me a party.

"Screw him," I say to myself, walking off.

"Screw this town, I hate this place," I look around but don't see my mother or John or Nan in the crowd yet. I'm so ready to get out of here.

I look up at the old red brick building that is Bayport-Blue Point High School and give it a middle finger salute and these parting words: "I'm going to show all of you. Watch me. I'm going to make something of myself. Just watch."

About a year later, I'm at Bates College. The school is located in Lewiston, Maine just over a forty-five minute drive north of Portland, and is often referred to as the "Bates Bubble," for its physical isolation and disconnect between the "preppy" college and the "townie" community. The campus quad paths are dotted with

---

1   Pseudonym.

charming black lamp-posts that stretch across a manicured lawn, where quaint New England-style red brick buildings and a gray stone nondenominational chapel have sat for a century or more. The thick, tall trees throughout the quad create a canopy of foliage, keeping the world outside at bay. It's spring and unseasonably warmer than usual. I'm walking along the path toward the house where I live. In my hand, I'm carrying a letter to the world, letting those I love know that I'm sorry for what I'm about to do.

I failed to meet my expectations for doing well in college; I was a borderline, almost failing student. Mr. Zornik's prediction was about to come true. I keep thinking to myself, there's no way I'm returning home a failure. When I arrive in my room, I place the letter on the table next to my bed. I take some rope I'd purchased earlier, stand up on my desk chair, tie the rope around a pipe running along the wall in the room, and loop a noose around my neck. I check to make sure I've done everything right, rechecking to make sure the rope is secured to the pipe, and take one last look at the letter on the bed, telling my mom I'm sorry, my Nan, everyone. Tears run down my cheeks. I close my eyes and kick the chair out from under me. My world gets hazy and goes dark.

I wake up on the floor, to the sound of my best friend, Andrew, pounding on the door, my head and neck throbbing, I'm confused by the scene around me: the noose around my neck, the chair tipped over, rope ripped from the pipe, pain in so many parts of my body.

Andrew pounds on the door some more, "I know you're in there, Joe. Open up, don't be hiding from me." He's been watching me deteriorate quickly, falling into a depression, and has increasingly become concerned about me. He never lets a day go by without checking in on me.

I yell as best as I can, "Be right there, let me get up."

"What the hell," I can hear him yelling as loud as he can so I can hear him through the door; my neighbors are used to this, "Did you sleep all day again? Open the door."

I grab the evidence and shove it under the bed, fixing the chair. I take my fleece vest I wear all the time, and zip it up over my neck. I look in the mirror before opening the door, and my head has multiple bruises forming so I try to think of something fast to tell Andrew.

I open the door and Andrew takes one look at me, saying, "What the HELL happened to your face?"

I try to diffuse his worry, "What? Are you saying I don't look pretty enough for you?"

He forcefully grabs my arm, "You're coming with me now."

I know I'm caught, and respond, "I'll go, if you promise to never tell anyone about this."

He looks at me, "Of course, you're my brother."

Andrew marches me to the health center, already panicking about what just happened. He spends the night with me at the clinic. I'm placed under twenty-four hour observation, staying there until they trust me enough to go back to my dorm. The agreement is they will not send me home, if I promise to follow through on my commitment to deal with my suicide attempt.

After I was back on the road to recovery, the very first thing the health center staff and Dean Branham did was give me the funds and transportation to travel to a highly recommended family-owned audiology clinic in Rockport, Maine, and purchase a hearing aid. I had not worn a hearing aid since early high school. I finished the school year on the Dean's list, writing letters of thanks to the health center staff (I'm very accident prone, so they got to know me pretty well over the years) and Dean Branham. Dean Branham writes back, saying, "it was your hard work and native intelligence" that deserves the credit for the success I found after getting the hearing aids. It's the first time that I ever heard someone refer to me as intellectually gifted.

I start to think, "Maybe I do belong here."

TWENTY

Dilemmas of the d/Deaf Superhero's Alter(nating) Ego

Often when we think of superheroes these names from the Justice League come to mind: Superman, Batman, Flash, Wonder Woman, Green Lantern. The myths of all superheroes are intimately associated with each comic book character, defining their origin story, life history, and identity. If you ask someone to tell you Superman's origin story, they'd reply with something about the superhero being born on the imminently doomed planet Krypton, crash landing a spaceship in farmland, and how he came to acquire and master his superpowers. Ask about his life history, they'd reply that he's a reporter, in love with Lois Lane, lives in Metropolis, his mentors were Jor-El and Lara, and his arch nemesis is Lex Luthor. They'd also tell you about kryptonite – the Superman universe version of Achilles' heel. For Superman's identity, the conversation would move naturally to his stumbling alter-ego, Clark Kent.

Geoff Klock (2002) writes in his decisive work on the superhero narrative that the comic genre deserves as much attention and respect as we give to works considered high culture. One of the paradoxes of the superhero narratives of late has been the addition of darker, more complex interpretations of heroes as superhero comics entered a "dark age." In the recent reimagining of the *Spider-Man 3* myth, a black symbiote (the alien suit) takes over Spiderman's costume, morphing not only his already extraordinary powers but also his personality. Klock's (2002) analysis of the movie *Unbreakable*, starring Samuel L. Jackson as Elijah Price a comic book fanatic who views the world through this medium, examines this blurring of the lines between the superhero/supervillain narratives, and the lessons of taking the superhero myth too far. Elijah, armed with his superhero epistemology, assumes that his brittle bones disease is proof of the comic book world axiom that we each possess a polarizing other who is our exact opposite. Klock (2002) writes, "It appears that *Unbreakable* is in the Jung-Campbell-Levi-Strauss lineage, as Elijah claims that superhero comic books are only exaggerations of an eternally true archetype of the hero that has always lived" (p. 179). Seeking his polar opposite, Elijah takes his superhero epistemology too far by staging major disasters to live (or prove) his superhero theory, ultimately leading to Elijah being sent to a mental health facility. Elijah's example makes me wonder if I, too, need to think about the sometimes fuzzy line between superhero and supervillain.

My favorite superhero is Spiderman. I like him the most because he is the only superhero I know of that is pathetic when not in the costume. Spiderman's alter-ego, Peter Parker, is a brooding, awkward adolescent who is shy, as opposed to Batman's uber-rich Bruce Wayne, Superman's charming journalist Clark Kent, or Wonder Woman's sharp boutique owner Diana Prince. Peter Parker is lonely, lacks confidence, feels remorse, and is often rejected by his peers as well as the adult world around him. The Spiderman/Peter Parker dualism seems to be more precisely representative of my own subaltern d/Deaf superhero alter(nating)ego. When Peter Parker switches to Spiderman, his personality changes even as his superpowers are not diminished whether costumed or not. This rings true for me too. When I put on the identity of subaltern Deaf superhero, my personality changes, and I have superhero strength to combat forces of audism/ableism. But on the days I do not wear my superhero identity, I'm vulnerable to the phonocentric world.

Phonocentric ideology (in)formed the social reality I lived in growing up with deafness, and I interpellated the majoritarian constructions of Hearingness and (dis)ability, attempting to make my deafness/disability disappear (both literally by hiding my hearing aids and figuratively by hiding my thoughts, feelings, and what I did and did not hear). Michael Apple (1990) observes, "Functionally, ideology has been evaluated historically as a form of false consciousness which distorts one's picture of social reality and serves the interests of the dominant classes in society" (p. 20). Building on Apple's idea of dominant classes (the phonocentric majoritarian society), I can see how a form of audist false consciousness distorts my own social reality (navigating a hearing-dominated world) by using concealment/hiding as a coping strategy for moments when phonocentrism moves stealthily into the core of my thinking. During moments of weakness, audist false consciousness distorts how I think about my identity.

The term "valedictorian of the retards," cleverly and cruelly created by my high school teacher, is a mirror image of our larger society's hearing-centered constructions of deafness, deaf children, and schooling. For this teacher, I was the token "deaf kid" that had been accepted to a highly competitive school. In his mind, I had duped the system that was supposed to put me in my rightful place, with the "retards."

There are several colonialist tricks here that we need to look at carefully. To start with, mental retardation is constructed as a categorical placeholder for those deemed unworthy based on narrow notions of intellect. As Danforth, Slocum, and Dunkle (2010) make clear, the myth that there is a population of people who sorely lack intellectual potential and that there is no use in attempting to educate them still rings true today. Danforth et al. (2010) explain pioneering learning disability scholars such as Samuel A. Kirk "proselytized" about what the authors term the "educability narrative" to counter dominant hereditarian myths of "a hierarchy of innate intellectual prowess across the population" being perpetuated by pre-World War II doctors and scientists (p. 12). However the tragedy of Kirk's efforts to use the "educability narrative" is how it left "mental retardation as a doubly-stigmatized remnant" when challenged to create a distinction between learning disability and mental retardation (p. 7). While Kirk's "educability narrative" provided a much needed boost to causes supporting the education of children with special needs, it came at a cost: the continuation of those with mental retardation deemed as unworthy and an institutional web-like system largely built as a place to hold them.

The *colonialist trick on me* here was that I bought into the audist/ableist rat-race of proving my worth intellectually (based on normative constructions of intelligence, ability, and identity). I also bought into the idea that I needed to dupe people to make my way in the world, that I needed to trick everyone into thinking I'm smart, able, and can "pass" as hearing. Even to this day, I feel this way despite knowing where these feelings come from. Some days, on really bad days, these feelings of failure win over. These are the days I conceal myself, my ideas, and my feelings from the world.

Dymaneke Mitchell (2006) in her article "Flashcard: Alternating between Visible and Invisible Identities" writes about the multiplicity of identity constructions and how they come to the surface based on context:

> My experiences of being African American, female, and deaf manifested like a flashcard. The visibility or invisibility of one of these identities usually incites the visibility or invisibility of the others. It is these moments of flashing that determine my reality. I live in the movements or spaces between these states of invisibility and visibility and/or femaleness, deafness, and blackness (p. 137).

If I were to apply the metaphor of flashcards to my own life history, it would be an alternating between my always already colonized self versus my empowered subaltern self. Mitchell (2006) explains that what is visible is her lived experiences, and what is invisible is how theoretical constructs "inform and shape" experiences. The theoretical construct that informed my worldview as a graduating senior was one of needing to "pass" as able-bodied and intelligent; this was my alter(nating) ego. I recognize that I come from a place of privilege; even as my mother identifies our roots as working class, I was raised with a sense of entitlement and often used this to fuel my counter attacks against the discursive systems that were trying to oppress me.

I thought by being accepted to Bates it would somehow give me the status, the right to claim my place in this world as someone who is smart, not just mediocre (or inferior). I thought I would show my abilities and "pass." Mr. Zornik's comment, while hurtful, was an example of the workings of phonocentric colonialism that made me want to push the boundaries of what was acceptable for a "deaf kid." I was on the path toward trying to be accepted in a hearing-centered world, or so I thought. I was accepting the colonial framework and "willingly" submitting to being ruled by audism/ableism, and normative constructions of Hearingness, ableness, and intellectual prowess. When I don't meet these constructions or become overwhelmed by them, I use the tactic I learned back in preschool – concealment. But by adulthood I learned a more sophisticated form of concealment and that is to hide. Hiding almost cost me my life at Bates.

The dilemma of the alter(nating) ego demonstrates the twofold paradox that even as my Deaf identity may come to the surface, as I navigate this world, my ego concurrently alters and alternates with my deaf colonized self. The ego (my identity) paradox is reminiscent of the Danteian inferno-like impasse, where sinful lovers (my identities as a deaf and/or Deaf man) spin in perpetual motion for eternity. My original sin of deafness (and growing up and living in a hearing-centered world) is what has put me in this phonocentric hell, and this is the place a Deaf subaltern escapes from once they move to counter-hegemonic tactics. But, for me, this escape is only ephemeral, sometimes fleeting; as I live in a hearing-dominated world, I am caught up in a minute-by-minute clash against phonocentric powers that seek to normalize and colonize me both through words and deeds. Growing up and living in a phonocentric world exacts a heavy price.

The dilemma that I face as a d/Deaf subaltern is the daily praxis of struggling, resisting, and transforming (as well as being aware and reflective of when accepting) this phonocentric colonialist world and its powerful, relentless forces that are trying to colonize me. This all started back in preschool, when the link between language (my hands) and power (audism) converged. I face the dilemma of the after-effects of linguicide and ethnocide, not being able to share in the world of sign with enough proficiency to participate fully in the Deaf subaltern dialogue through ASL and engage other Deaf people with our natural language.

I think back to the pain I felt when I met Laurel, not being able to communicate with her. I remember the shame that crept into me. While exchanging e-mails with Laurel about the day we met, she hits on exactly what I'm thinking, writing, "I remember I thought it was VERY interesting the fact that we are both deaf and you don't know any sign language. My supervisor Catherine [a hearing person] interpreted for us!!!"

We exchanged a few more e-mails about that day, and Laurel then asked me to send the vignette about getting my hands slapped in preschool that I brought up during one exchange. She fired back an e-mail within minutes, almost stream-of-conscious:

> I was a student at Clarke School for the Deaf for three years- are you familiar with that school? its a strict ORAL school- no waving hands or gesturing (they call it signing because none of us there knew ASL or how to sign) allowed...we were all required to use our voice all the time...on my first day of school at Clarke I got lost and couldn't find my dorm...I saw a deaf girl who was a Clarke student and I asked (talked) to her (no signing or gesturing) where was Bell Hall Dorm and she couldn't understand me. I repeated the question few times and still she couldn't understand me. Then I gestured (at that time I was 13 and didn't know ANY sign language) "where-sleep?") and she immediately understood me and showed me where the dorm was...a staff saw me gesturing and pulled my arm inside the school building and placed me in the corner...and told me to look straight at the corner for one hour...I asked why and she said I was using my hands to talk the girl...I tried to explain to her why I was signing with my hands because I was lost...she refused to listen to me and left...I cried so hard and at that

time I didn't understand what I was doing so wrong...and why I was being punished...in my mind I thought I was punished because I was lost??? Or they can do whatever they want to do with me after my mother left?? I cried so hard and became soo homesick.

As I read her e-mail, I think back to the first time I met Laurel. I remember the initial feelings of kinship and fantasy I had about her being a like-minded radical for Deaf culture. I thought she would agree with my position that technology infringes and disenfranchises people with deafness by spreading a discourse that discursively works to normalize the failing deaf body. When she showed me her cochlear implants, Laurel ruptured not only my fantasy of her, but my fantasy of Deaf culture: either someone is oral deaf or culturally Deaf. Meeting Laurel that day made me understand that the battle lines between the two camps were more blurred than I'd thought.

I think back to my meeting Laurel as representative of the many moments of epiphanies that I've experienced along this journey that is this book and my life. Laurel is the last sign-only teacher in her school, and identifies herself intimately with Deaf culture, and yet she has a cochlear implant. At that time, in my view she was part Deaf subaltern superhero and part audist subject. Or, in terms of comic book mythology, the black symbiote (the alien suit) of phonocentric colonialism had taken over a Deaf subaltern superhero. I too had fallen under the spell of phonocentric hegemony. Under this costume the virtuous self-ego struggles to break free. Laurel and I are like Spiderman, who was able to defeat the black symbiote with his inherent morality.

Understanding the workings of phonocentric hegemony requires an unmasking of how colonial regimes perpetuate the cycle of audist oppression and subjugation. The making of deaf people into subjects is a process in which the subjects themselves participate in the hegemonic (re)production of phonocentric colonialism. Antonio Gramsci's (2005) concepts of hegemony and counter-hegemony provide a critical framing of the plight of a subaltern who must be enlightened (and possibly disciplined) enough to work outside these discursive systems. Julie Kaomea (2003) explains that with the Gramscian conception of hegemony, the "ruling classes achieve domination not by force or coercion alone but also by creating subjects who "willingly" submit to being ruled" (p. 23). For me, a Deaf subaltern superhero is not just one who is subordinated, but one who also works outside the colonizing ideological framework to agitate the status quo of structures that oppress d/Deaf community members.

Paulo Freire (1985) notes, "No oppressive order could permit the oppressed to begin to question: Why?" (p. 67). I've always felt the need to hide and "pass" because societal discrimination fed me the perception that deafness/disability is a deficit (making a direct correlation between intellect and dis/ability). The individual with a deafness/disability is forced by these discursive systems to assume that there must be something inherently different and, sometimes even, wrong with their body or themselves. Freire (1985) reasons, "Translated into practice, this concept is well suited to the purposes of the oppressors, whose tranquility rests on how well people fit the world the oppressors have created, and how little they question it" (Freire, p. 57). The colonialist trick, again, is that it masks any focus on society's prejudgment of those with deafness/disabilities as not problematic.

During the time I was at Bates, I gradually developed some critical, reflective ways of thinking about myself and the world around me. It was at Bates that I started to confront my past with my developing alter(nating) ego. As a young man with working class roots, raised from seven on by my mother and grandmother, the world as I'd understood it up to that point was vastly different than what I was seeing around me. It was a world juxtaposed between learning about critical ways of thinking while living and learning with classmates who came from a world of privilege that I'd never known existed. My first exposure to critical and social justice issues was through the lens of class privilege in the classroom and in the dorms where I lived. The first years, I hid from my professors; I hid from the letters saying I was on academic probation, instead seeking solace in friends that were in my first-year center. I partied my way through the pain of knowing that I was failing. I no longer had a hearing aid, and could not afford one, so I struggled alone with my thoughts of failure in a hearing-dominated world, keeping them inside until that one fateful day in the spring, when I snapped.

These are the dilemmas of living this life.

I want to get back to earlier when Joe Tobin referred to my life story, struggling against audism/ableism, as somewhat similar to the story of the comic book and action movie superhero with a disability Daredevil. My identity (re)formations and life story resemble the hero archetype and quest-like journey to discover my own potential and superhero powers, owing in part to having lived life with deafness. Petra Kuppers (2006) writes:

> Daredevil is a dark superhero, in the Batman vein. He became disabled as a child, when he ran into a vat of acid. He is blind, but, like many disabled super-heroes, he is a supercrip: he has the ability to 'see' by focusing on sound waves washing over his environment. This incredibly heightened sensory access allows him to swing freely across the rooftops and canyons of New York, his particular Gotham, save people, and punish perpetrators as obsessively as Batman did (p. 91).

I, too, see myself like Daredevil and Batman in that I'm a dark superhero. I became deaf because the emergency room doctor trivialized my mother's concerns for my health as a newborn, dismissing my health, and instead diagnosing my mom as a hysterical woman. But this is where I part company with Kuppers' use of the term supercrip; I do not see myself as a supercrip. Linda Ware (2002) defines supercrip saying, "the term is intentionally 'in-your-face' in an attempt to minimize the ubiquitous 'overcoming' narrative depicted in media and film" (p. 164). Ware (2002) explicates the discursive workings of the term supercrip and how:

> These "supercrip" stories, according to poet and author Eli Clare (1999), reinforce the superiority of the nondisabled body and rely upon the perception that "disability and achievement contradict each other and that any disabled person who overcomes this contradiction is heroic" (8). Clare's disability counternarrative offers no apology for mixing politics with the personal as she insists that the "dominant story about disability should be about abelism, not the inspirational supercrip crap, the believe-it-or-not disability story" (2). (p. 144)

Supercrip crap is a hegemonic discourse that perpetuates the need for people with disabilities to focus on their "difference"; the narrative focus is on "overcoming," which would suggest that being deaf is something one must overcome. Kathleen McDougall (2007) writes about the dichotomizing phenomenon of "ag shame" (which she explains is a South African idiomatic expression that means something like "non-entity") and "superheroes" in her research on South African constructions of disability and issues of agency:

> Herein lies one possibility of recovering agency. If the implications here is to be 'ag shamed' is to be attached to, and defined by, a disabling narrative of innocent damage, the corollary is that one can choose to participate in authoring that narrative, or choose not to, or write the narrative differently... (p. 390)

Now it is time to reverse the lens, back onto the audist/ableist cultural climate that makes being "different" so difficult. For me, there is the danger of reading my life story as the supercrip crap that is perpetuated by mass media and audist/ableist discourses. I do not want my life story to be read as an "overcoming" of my "disability." I want my life story to inform and critique how we think about (dis)ability, deafness, and schooling. As I've said earlier, I see this superhero version of myself as a strategy in the tradition of counter-discourses and counter-storytelling used by marginalized communities (e.g., Ladd, 2003, 2005; Mutua and Swadener, 2004; Ladson-Billings and Tate, 2006; Delgado and Stefanic, 2001; Solarzano and Yasso, 2002) to counter the discursive workings of audist/ableist oppression and subjugation.

Our society wants to make the disability disappear; our society wants to make the disability narrative about supercrip crap to take over the more radical, groundbreaking subaltern discourses that challenge the core audist/ableist belief system that people with deafness/disabilities need to conform to normative constructions of ability.

The failing, unruly body must be normalized, even if by illusion, with prosthesis (in my case, hearing aids or cochlear implants for young deaf children today) as Mitchell and Snyder (2000) write, "In a literal sense a prosthesis seeks to accomplish an illusion. A body deemed lacking, unfunctional, or inappropriately functional needs compensation, and prosthesis helps to effect this end...The judgment that a mechanism is faulty is always already profoundly social" (p. 6). Rather than focus on the "overcoming" through the use of hearing aids, which only reinforces the construction that I need to normalize my always already failing ears, I want to offer a counter reading in the context of my own life history of Kuppers' (2006) final, insightful comments, that Daredevil has "this incredibly heightened sensory access [that] allows him to swing freely across the rooftops and canyons of New York, his particular Gotham, save people, and punish perpetrators as obsessively as Batman did" (p. 91). I see my own life history and superpowers somewhat similarly.

But for me, these superpowers are not heightened senses; instead my superpowers are my heightened sensitivity to the impositions of schooling on young deaf children, who are navigating the tricky waters of phonocentric colonialism. I possess anger against the discursive systems that oppressed me, that are oppressing young deaf children today. Another superhero power that I cultivated during my years growing up in a hearing-dominated world was storytelling. I want to "punish perpetrators" with superpowerful stories that move people to act, to push the phonocentric colonialist discourse back. Usually supercrip depicts extraordinary bodily and mental powers, working to overcome what the world judges that same body lacks. My updated version of the *Supercrip* battles not only for physiological functioning but also for social justice. The supervillains in this version of Supercrip are not broken ears but destructive social structures and their processes that systemically harm children whose bodies and minds do not conform to narrow-minded cultural scripts of dis/ability. These supervillainous structures need to be toppled.

My journey has been a slow crossing to get to where I am today. My studies and travels would reach a life history apex in my rousing conversation with Dr. I. King Jordan, the first Deaf president of Gallaudet and an iconic figure in Deaf culture, leading to the long road toward becoming a Deaf subaltern researcher and storyteller. What I learned at Bates would lead me on a six-year adventure before coming to graduate school at Arizona State University, and meeting my two mentors, Joe Tobin and Beth Blue Swadener, who would show me how to apply decolonizing tactics to my own life story.

TWENTY-ONE

The A-Team and Rescuing Emma from the Second Graders

At first there is confusion.

A blinding light shines into the windows that run the length of our fifth-grade classroom. There are two bullhorn blares so thunderous the ground below our feet quakes. My hearing aid feels like it's going to burst. I can see outside the window a van steering out of control on the nearby schoolyard and playground.

Our teacher, Mr. Bradley screams, Watch out! Everybody get out of the way!

I watch from my desk a speeding black van with a red GMC logo and full front bullbars on the grille barreling toward me. Even as the headlights are on highbeam I keep watching and don't look away – I'm glued to the action. The van crashes through the windows, exploding glass and brick into the classroom. It skids and slides about 180 degrees until it pulls to a stop just before my desk.

Quickly I take in and process the scene in front of me. The black GMC van with its red and black turbine-style wheels; a thick red stripe that angles across the body of the van; the rooftop spoiler. It comes to me all of the sudden: It's the A-Team!

Almost on cue, The A-Team theme song plays and the side-door of the van opens with Faceman, Murdock, Hannibal, and Mr. T. They jump from the van onto my classroom floor. Debris from the crash is everywhere; desks are overturned; exhaust smoke and dust fill the air. The A-Team lines up in front of the van, they look around as kids from my class scurry for cover. All my classmates are in shock. Mr. Bradley is in shock too. None of us can believe it.

FACEMAN: I'm looking for Joey Valente.

JOEY: I'm right over here, Faceman. This is totally rad.

FACEMAN: Joey, they're coming for us. They've tracked all of us down and now they're coming for you too. You need to come with us right away.

JOEY: Who's coming for us?

MR. BRADLEY: Who are you? How dare you crash your van into our classroom and interrupt our social studies lesson!

MR. T: I ain't gonna wait for this fool!

MR. BRADLEY: I know you! You're that wrestler, right? Mr. Z, yes?

MR. T: Who this fool? I'm gonna get you, sucker! Hannibal, we on the jazz?

HANNIBAL: Everybody relax. What's your name, sir?

JOEY: That's Mr. Bradley, my teacher, Hannibal. Mr. Bradley, I have to go now. The A-Team is here for me, okay?

MR. BRADLEY: You will do no such thing, Joey. Stay put. I'm going to call down to the main office and have the principal, Mr. Weik, handle this. You're all in trouble. I know that for sure. Just stay right where you are Alphabet-Team.

MURDOCK: A-Team! We're the A-Team. Ah…just forget him. Let's go! Joey jump in the truck! Hurry!

MR. BRADLEY: Joey, stay right there. Do not move. I'm calling the main office right now.

HANNIBAL: Make your decision, son. What will it be? You coming or staying?

JOEY: I don't know. I don't want to get in trouble with Mr. Weik. He's the principal.

FACEMAN: Joey, didn't you write us a letter?

JOEY: Yes, but I didn't know you guys would come get me like this. This is –

MR. BRADLEY: – Joey, what is this all about? You are the reason for all this?

FACEMAN: Joey, come on. You said in your letter that you needed us to help you escape. You said Mr. Bradley was boring and school was boring. You said you needed us to come and break you out of school.

MR. BRADLEY: You think I'm boring? How dare –

JOEY: No, no, Mr. Bradley you're a nice guy and all. I don't want to hurt your feelings. It's just I sit here all day and do nothing. I can never hear nothing. I sit here all day and pretend I hear what's going on. But I never do.

MR. BRADLEY: What do you mean you do nothing? You do school.

MR. T: Come on, you guys suckers? Don't listen to this fool! We gotta get out of here, the police are coming.

JOEY: I don't want to do school no more, Mr. Bradley. I want be an action-hero like The A-Team and help people and drive around the country in a van. That's the life, Mr. Bradley.

HANNIBAL: Okay, we're done here. Coming or going? Come, jump in the van now!

JOEY: Bye, Mr. Bradley! Bye!

MR. BRADLEY: Joey, Joey, Joey…stop daydreaming…you're not going anywhere…

Hu? I say.

You were daydreaming, again, Joey, Mr. Bradley says, You're not going anywhere, you need to get back to work on your social studies worksheets.

Okay, Mr. Bradley, I say, wiping away the blur from my eyes.

I really thought the A-Team came to help me escape. Ugh, I think to myself, this sucks, I'm still in school. I look at the clock. It is only 9:17 a.m. now? Darn, school takes forever. I'm so bored. I hate school. School sucks.

Sean sits right across from me. He looks at me, rolls his eyes like I'm ridiculous, says, Man, yu really spazzed out there for a long time. I kept try'n to tell yu not to go off to La-La Land. You keep doing it. If you dun't finish yur workshit yur not gonna be able to do Safety Patrol today.

Ugh, I groan.

The classroom phone rings. My hearing aid picks up static first, then there is this short bursts of ring-ring-ring – the feedback pierces my ears. No pain, no gain. When that phone rings it may hurt but it's also a call for freedom. It rings so rarely. But when it does, it's a call from the main office to have a student go somewhere or it's a call from the specials teacher for everybody to go to gym, music, library or art – that we've been rescheduled. I look up; I pray it's the office calling for me because my mom's here to take me out of school early; if not, I hope it's Mrs. Kapell's speech class or Mrs. Cadillac's resource room I have to go to – just anything to escape the boredom of school.

Mr. Bradley walks briskly across the room to the phone to answer it.

Hello?! Mr. Bradley says.

Everybody listens.

Mr. Bradley says, Yes, yes, uh-hu. Okay. Yes. Uh-hu. Okay. Thanks, Doris, tell Mrs. Cadillac we're going to get this right soon enough.

He hangs the phone up and scans the room. We all hold our breathes with hope and anticipation.

Mr. Bradley's eyes settle on me.

Yes! I celebrate with a fist pump in the air.

Okay, Joey, let's go, Mr. Bradley says, Mrs. Cadillac says you were supposed to be at resource room today at 9 a.m. and you're late. We spoke to you about this already. You go twice a day at 9 a.m. and 2 p.m. on Mondays, Wednesdays, and Fridays. On Tuesdays and Thursdays you go twice a day at 8:45 a.m. and 1:45 p.m., okay? Remember? Don't forget – then you have Mrs. Kapell for speech therapy once a day, every day now after lunch at 11:30, okay? I know you are big enough now to remember all this. Now hurry up. Get going to Mrs. Cadillac's. Bring your social studies worksheet and tell Mrs. Cadillac about the spelling quiz we're having this Friday and the book report that is due next week. Okay?

Yes, I say, Okay, Mr. Bradley. But he stands in front of the door, blocking my exit.

Oh, one more thing. You didn't tell me what book you're taking out from the library for the book report. Which one is it again?

Encyclopedia Brown, I say.

Mr. Bradley asks, Which one?

All of them—the whole series, I say.

How many is that? He asks.

Sixteen, I answer.

He squints his eyes, You are going to write a book report about *all sixteen* of them? Or are you going to *read* all of them and write about *one* book?

I answer, I'm reading and writing a book report about all of them. I want to read all sixteen in the series. We have them all in the library. I only have five left to go.

Mr. Bradley just shakes his head. Like he doesn't understand. Doesn't say anything back. He does smile like he knows something I don't. He has a goofy way of smiling with his eyes; you can see him rolling them behind his thick glasses. When he does this, it means he's trying to tease you. Mr. Bradley is a real big teaser. He doesn't just make fun of kids, he also makes fun of teachers, the secretaries in the main office, the janitors, and Mr. Weik too.

I look at him and eye the door, Can I go now? I'm going to be late.

Oh, yes, Mr. Bradley says, Go, go ahead, get going, you're already late.

He moves out of the way for me to leave. I get to the bottom of the stairwell and realize I forgot my social studies worksheet, spelling book, and the last five *Encyclopedia Brown* books left I have to read for my book reports. So I have to go back up to my class and get all the stuff.

But before I get to the top of the stairs, I see Emma. Emma has Down syndrome; everybody says she has Downs, for short. I didn't know what this meant when we first met because we were best friends in Mrs. Kapell's speech class in kindergarten and first grade. We both repeated kindergarten together and were always partners in Mrs. Cadillac's resource room for board games. I love Emma because she is always so happy to see me. Except now we never get to see each other anymore. Emma is in a different, smaller class now.

When I see Emma in the hallway, I worry she is wandering again. She's always getting in trouble for that. Emma is known for stopping by everyone's class to say "Hi" and give hugs. Emma sees me right away and comes down the stairs toward me.

She's very excited, Hi, Joey!

Hi, Emma, I say.

How yu doin' Joey?

She leans in to give me a hug on the stairs. I'm taller by a foot almost so she goes one step up and puts her head in my chest, wrapping her arms around me tight like I'm a tall tree.

Emma repeats, Did yu hear me Joey? Did yu see my lips Joey? Look at my lips, okay? I say: How yu doin' Joey?

Doin' good, Emma, where yu supposed to be, Emma?

I'm goin' to the bathroom, Joey. She gets annoyed I'm asking her where she is supposed to be and gives me the look like "come on leave me alone."

Emma, yu just passed the bathroom, it's at the top of the stairs, I say.

Oh, Emma says, I saw yu so I wanted to say, Hi.

I say, Yu don't have a bathroom pass. Who's yur teacher?

Oh, Emma says, she ignores my question and looks away up the stairs.

I say, Come on, Emma, let me take yu back to class before yu get in trouble.

Okay, she says, Come, Joey, I have to go the bathroom first, okay?

Okay, Emma, I say, I'll go with you.

We walk up the stairs to the bathroom. I wait outside for Emma to finish up in the girl's room so I can walk her back to class. She takes a really long time. I yell into the bathroom, Emma, come on, hurry up!

Emma comes out of the bathroom.

I say, Come on, I'm going to be so late for Mrs. Cadillac's class. I ask again, Who 're yu suppos'd to be with right now?

Emma says, I'm supposed to be with Mr. Dornhoffer.

Oh, I say, Okay, let's go.

Wait! Emma yells.

What? I say.

We got to say hi to Mrs. Kapell first, Emma says.

Emma, I say, Come on! Yu need to get back to class. Yu know Mrs. Kapell is goin' to be mad at yu for bein' in the halls again.

Joey, Emma says, Yu're no fun.

Fine, I say, Do whatever yu want. I'm goin' to Mrs. Cadillac's class before I get into more trouble. Bye.

I take off down the hallway.

I walk down the stairs and see Emma follow behind me. Mrs. Cadillac's class is on the other side of school, down the BOCES special ed hallway where they keep all the much older kids and adults in wheel chairs that drool on themselves. For some reason, the lights never work in this hallway so it's always dark. Everybody in the school is scared to come down this way because it smells like diapers and the BOCES kids are here. Nobody wants to be caught here.

Emma keeps following me. She stays a few feet behind me. Emma pretends that she is sneaking up behind me. Every time I look back Emma freezes as if she is invisible. Finally, I look back and say, Emma, I can see yu following me. Go to class!

She giggles a bit. But doesn't turn around. She keeps following.

I say it again, Emma, yu really need to get back to class.

Emma says, Bye! She runs off to the far staircase that no one uses.

I stand in front of Mrs. Cadillac's door trying to decide if I should go in or chase after Emma.

I decide to go in.

When I walk through the door, Mrs. Cadillac says, Well, Joey, I thought you'd never show up. Everything okay? I was just about to have the main office call Mr. Bradley.

Yes, Mrs. Cadillac, everything is fine.

Why you so late? Mrs. Cadillac asks.

I had to go to the bathroom really bad, I say.

Oh, okay, she says.

Mrs. Cadillac walks over to me. I go to put my stuff in my cubby. It's then that I realize I forgot to bring my social studies worksheet, spelling book, and *Encyclopedia Brown* books.

Ugh, I say.

What? Mrs. Cadillac asks.

I forgot my workbook and stuff in Mr. Bradley's class, I say.

Alright, Joey, go get them. Hurry up. No more bathroom breaks. Hurry.

Yes, Mrs. Cadillac, I'll be right back.

I go out the classroom door and head for the same staircase Emma went up – the one no one ever uses – the Slow Stairs. Everyone knows to stay away from the Slow

Stairs or risk being made fun of. I take those stairs anyway. I figure if I saw Emma walking around I could take her back to class on my way to get my books.

When I get to the top of the stairwell, I see three girls surrounding Emma. I don't know their names but I know they're from Mrs. Connelly's second-grade class.

Emma is excited to see me. She says, Joey, let me show you my new friends.

I'm annoyed with Emma. Why isn't she back in class already?

All three of the girls look like they're wearing the same exact outfits: pink coveralls and pink Converse sneakers. They whisper to each other and giggle.

I walk up to Emma, say, What yu doin'?

Emma doesn't answer. She's distracted by the girls whispering to each other. So I look over to them. They look at Emma and me and start laughing and whispering.

I look to Emma. Emma looks to me. Neither of us knows why they're laughing.

I ask, Why yu laughin'?

One of the girls with a pigtail turns around and says, Oh, nothing.

No, I say, Why yu laughin'?

One of the girls with blonde hair acts all phony sweet and says, Oh, really, it's nothing.

All three of the girls go back to talking.

They whisper. They giggle, again.

This time I hear something, just a small piece: Slow Stairs.

I wonder if they're saying something about us being on the Slow Stairs.

I ask them, Hey, hey, yu sayin' somethin' 'bout the Slow Stairs?

All three girls giggle and huddle together again. This time I hear everything:

He must be slow like Emma.

All three girls laugh.

Hey! I yell at them. Who yu call'n slow?

They ignore me. I look at Emma. Emma just shrugs her shoulders and says, They are my new friends Joey.

I get mad at Emma, I say, No Emma, they're not yur friends.

The girl with pigtails pretends to whisper but yells really loud, I bet Deaf kid and Emma are boyfriend and girlfriend.

I say, We 'ar not!

The girl with the blonde hair starts singing first and then the other two join in:

Deaf kid and 'Tard sitting in a tree,

K-I-S-S-I-N-G,

First comes love,

Then comes marriage,

Then comes Corky in a baby carriage,

Sucking his thumb,

Wetting his pants,

Doing the hula-hula dance.

Emma shrieks in delight and claps her hands, I love singing! I love singing!

No, no, Emma, I say, Emma, they're making fun of us.

All three girls laugh and laugh and laugh.

What happened next I can't be too sure. All I know is that I kept hearing Emma say, Joey, stop fighting; Joey, stop fighting; Joey, stop fighting.

When the gym teacher, Mr. Stiggerwald, finally pulls me away from two second-grade girls I was standing over and punching, I realize I had lost it. I'm completely enraged and dazed.

I look around and see the other second-grade girl with pigtails on the floor, nursing her elbows, knees, and head. All three of the girls have scratches and bruises already. There are also bruises on my knuckles and fingers.

Mr. Stiggerwald says, Joey, what did you do?

Emma stands up and runs over to me, gives me a hug, says, Joey are you okay? You shouldn't fight, Joey.

Mr. Stiggerwald looks at Emma, asks, Emma — what happened here?

Emma says, Joey fights them.

I can see that, Mr. Stiggerwald says. He looks at me, Joey, why are you beating up second-grade girls? That's not a fair fight. You're a boy and you're in fifth grade.

I say, They were making fun of Emma and me.

Why didn't you just go and get some help, Joey? Mr. Stiggerwald asks.

Because there was no time, Mr. Stiggerwald.

Mr. Weik, the principal shows up. He surveys the scene and says, What is this?

Mr. Stiggerwald doesn't allow me to answer. He answers for me, Joey beat up these poor second graders! A fifth-grade boy beating up second-grade girls.

Mr. Weik's face turns white and he notices my hearing aid on the floor by the stairwell. It must have fallen off when I was fighting with the girls. He walks over to the hearing aid and picks it up to hand to me. He says, Joey, is this true?

Yes, I say. I put the hearing aid in my ear.

Joey, Mr. Weik, says, You beat up second graders? I know you are a good kid. Why would you do something like that? You are the Captain of the Safety Patrol Team.

I start to worry I will lose my job as Captain or worse get kicked off the Safety Patrol Team entirely.

Emma pushes herself between Mr. Weik and me, Hi, Mr. Weik!

She gives Mr. Weik a hug.

Hi, Emma, are you involved in this too? Mr. Weik looks like he is becoming even more confused.

Mr. Stiggerwald says, Mr. Weik, Joey here beat up these poor second graders. Don't you think we should call his mother, maybe even the police?

Mr. Weik seems annoyed with Mr. Stiggerwald, You know, Chuck, why don't you go help those second graders to the nurse's office and get those bruises checked. Thanks.

Okay, come on kids, Mr. Stiggerwald says, Let's go, come on, get up, I'll walk you all down to Nurse Nancy's office.

Come with me Joey and Emma, Mr. Weik says.

We follow him. Emma doesn't seem to realize how much trouble we're in right now. All she keeps doing is saying "hi" to everybody we pass in the hallways, in the main office, and to Mr. Weik's secretary I call Mrs. Weik. She always gets mad at me when I call her Mrs. Weik for some reason.

Emma plops down on the leather chair. I stand next to her.

Mr. Weik says, You can sit, Joey. He walks around his desk and sits in his big leather chair.

No, thanks, I say.

Why don't you both tell me exactly what happened, Mr. Weik says.

I say, Those second graders were making fun of Emma and me.

Is that true, Emma? Mr. Weik looks to her.

Hi, Mr. Weik, she says.

Hi, Emma, Mr. Weik is very patient. He looks at her again, Emma, did those second graders make fun of you?

No, Emma says.

Oh, so what happened then?

Mr. Weik doesn't wait for an answer, he just gets up. He leans out his door to say something to Mrs. Weik, I guess.

When he turns around, he repeats his question: Emma, did those girls make fun of you?

No, she says, They're my friends.

Mrs. Weik comes into the room and looks at Emma, Honey, come with me. We're going to see Nurse Nancy.

Hi, Mrs. Tranny! Emma seems so excited again. I realize that the secretary's name is not Mrs. Weik.

You're not Mrs. Weik? I ask.

No, she says, My name is Mrs. Tranny. Joey, I've told you this before.

Sorry, I say.

Okay, we'll be back in a minute, Mrs. Tranny says, And, oh, I almost forgot Mr. Weik — I called Joan Kapell like you asked, she'll be down here in a minute.

Thanks, Mrs. Tranny, Mr. Weik says.

Mr. Weik turns to me now and asks, Joey, tell me what happened from the beginning, please.

I look to Mr. Weik and ask, Will I lose my Captain's badge, Mr. Weik?

Joey, Mr. Weik says, I don't know about that. Right now we need to figure out what happened here.

I beat them up Mr. Weik, I say.

Why would you beat up second graders Joey, they are so much smaller than you, Mr. Weik seems confused.

I say, Mrs. Kapell says I can fight them.

Just then, Mrs. Kapell comes into the room.

Hi, Mrs. Kapell, I say.

Hi, Joey, she says, Hi, Mr. Weik.

Mrs. Kapell always makes everything better so I'm so happy she is here.

Mr. Weik says, Have a seat Mrs. Kapell. Joey and I were just talking. He said you said he could fight...? Is that correct?

Mrs. Kapell says, I'm not so sure I know what we're talking about here.

Mr. Weik says, Well, Joey here says that he can fight second graders because you said so. Is that correct, Joey?

Mrs. Kapell wears a confused face. She looks at me for a clue. I don't have one to offer. I'm not too sure what is happening either.

Mr. Weik, Mrs Kapell asks, Can you fill me in on what's happening here?

Mr. Weik says, Joey beat up some second graders and he says he was allowed to because you said it was okay. Do I have that right, Joey?

Yes and no, I say, Mrs. Kapell — I look to her — They were making fun of us.

No, Mrs. Kapell says, I didn't tell Joey to fight. What's this someone making fun of Joey and Emma?

Okay, Mr. Weik says, I didn't think Mrs. Kapell would tell you to fight Joey.

I catch Mr. Weik smiling to Mrs. Kapell. I start to wonder if they are playing some game with me. Mr. Weik's face gets serious-looking real fast again. He says, You were going to say, Mrs. Kapell?

Mrs. Kapell says, Well, Joey and I were discussing the other day what to do if somebody were to — how does it go, Joey?

— call me out, I say.

Joey and I were discussing what to do if someone were to "call him out" to fight. Mrs. Kapell tells Mr. Weik.

Mr. Weik asks, What did you advise him to do?

Mrs. Kapell says, I told him fighting was forbidden but self-defense was not.

Mr. Weik looks to me, Was that what you were doing, Joey? Were you defending yourself against those second graders?

No, I say.

Oh, Mr. Weik says. He seems disappointed.

He asks again, They didn't try to hurt you?

No, I say, They tried to hurt Emma.

Mr. Weik seems confused again.

He looks at me, So you were fighting for Emma?

No, I say, I was self-defending Emma.

TWENTY-TWO

The Long Road from Gallaudet to Meeting of the Mentors

After graduating from Bates College, I wander aimlessly from job to job up and down the east coast, finally settling outside Washington, D.C., freelancing as a technical writer for various corporate, academic, and non-profit entities seeking federal funding, even occasionally dabbling in some ghost writing for airline travel magazines. It's the closest I've ever felt to being a real writer, and I'm making good money. I have so much debt from school that my work schedule is from five in the morning until ten or so most nights. My other best friend from Bates, Patrick, lives nearby but both of us work too much to spend time together. I'm mooching off his parents, Helga and Oz, who are like second parents to me. They spoil me with dinner waiting when I get home late, spend time sitting around talking with me, and generally treating me as if I were one of their children. One Sunday late in the spring, I wake up, put in my hearing aid, and hear nothing.

I think to myself, no big deal, I'll change the battery. I put in a new battery, nothing. I put in another, then another. Nothing. I start to realize that I can't even hear with the little residual hearing I do have. I turn on my clock radio as loud as I can to test my ears. I hear nothing. I go to the bathroom, try to clean out wax. Nothing. Now I know something's wrong. It's not my hearing aids or the batteries. I'm deaf. I walk upstairs to find Helga and Oz, they're in the kitchen, preparing my breakfast. I stand there watching the both of them move around the kitchen, not noticing my presence; Oz is cleaning pans at the sink, Helga cooking on the stove. Surely there must be noise, I think. I hear nothing.

I speak, "Hi." My mouth moves, but my ears don't hear my voice.

Oz and Helga turn around to look at me. Their mouths move. And, their mouths keep moving. No sound comes from their mouths, though.

Finally, frustrated, I say, "I'm deaf."

Oz says something.

I counter, unsure what he said, trying so hard to read his lips, "I can't hear anything."

I can see Helga mouth something looking like "hearing aid," then she smiles and points to her ears.

I explain to them, "I can't hear, even with the aids on. I'm deaf. I can't here anything at all. Not like I used to."

The next day, Oz and Helga won't let me drive to the doctor, so Patrick takes me. When we arrive, I realize that I had forgotten to put in my medical insurance paperwork, so they send us away until we fix it. It's not an emergency because I don't feel any pain, so we don't head to the emergency room or hospital. I schedule an appointment for a clinic that serves the uninsured, but have to wait over a week. In the meantime, I lose my clients because I can't communicate with them. But I don't care. I feel relief! I'm finally completely deaf. No longer in-between.

It seems almost like this is a divine intervention, especially with Gallaudet University nearby. So, despite Oz and Helga's strict orders not to drive until after I see the doctor, I visit Gallaudet while they're at work.

I arrive in the midst of a recruiting event. As I walk through the campus, watching students sign to one another, it seems surreal. I've entered the Deaf-World I've been reading about for so long.

I figure out where I'm supposed to go, heading through some buildings, where the event is being held. When I arrive, a recruiter, who speaks and signs, asks me why I'm here. So I tell him that I'm interested in pursuing my graduate degree.

We chitchat for some time, but it's tough because I can't sign or hear. I'm thankful when he goes off to talk with another recruit because I recognize a face across the room I've seen so many times before in books, newspapers, magazines, and on television: Dr. I. King Jordan, the first Deaf president of Gallaudet University. I get up my courage and walk over. The timing is perfect; he's now standing alone.

"Hi," I say, extending my hand.

Dr. Jordan shakes my hand, nods his head, signing and speaking, he says, "Hi, What's your name?"

"Joe," I say rather sheepishly, feeling worried he's going to judge me for not being able to sign. Worried too that I can only read lips, trying to be conscious I'm not invading his space in my attempts to understand.

"What brings you here, Joe?" He seems way too kind for what I think to be a celebrity. Dr. Jordan actually seems interested in meeting me.

"Well," I stumble, unsure what to say in what I know will be a short conversation before someone takes his attention away, "I guess, I sort of had an epiphany."

He looks at me, eyes to eyes, "What kind?"

I get so nervous, I spill everything out as quickly as I can: I tell him how much I've pined to become a part of Deaf culture, learn ASL, I want to do something – contribute something to the Deaf-World.

Dr. Jordan's mouth turns into a knowing smile, like he's heard this story so many times before. I know he has. He looks at me, puts his hand on my arm to show he understands all these built up emotions, and says these words to me before someone whisks him off for his keynote, "Welcome home."

I leave Gallaudet knowing for sure that I'm going to contribute something. I just don't know how, yet.

When I finally do meet up with the doctor, I find out I have an assortment of ear infections, allergies, and minor issues that can be cleared up with some medicine and time. I'm disappointed. I wanted out of the hearing-world rat race. Quickly, I come to the realization I'm without any work, and my debt is strangling me financially. So I do like most children do when overwhelmed, I call home to my mom.

She agrees to help me get my teaching degree, if I stop mooching off Oz and Helga and come home to New York. I feel like there's no choice now that I'm out of work, so I make plans to go to Columbia University to pursue my degree in deaf education while I support myself by teaching in the city.

I leave the city after one year of teaching, disenchanted with the public school system and its inept bureaucracy. When plans for funding at Columbia fall through, I move on to Phoenix where the cost of living and teacher salaries are advantageous, hoping I can go to school at Arizona State University, which is also much cheaper with in-state tuition. After another year of teaching, I secure a job working in the college of education at ASU, slowly but surely working my way through courses, first as a non-degree seeking student, and then on toward a doctorate in early childhood education. About a year into my doctoral coursework, I meet my first mentor on what would be this journey, Dr. Beth Blue Swadener.

One of my first memories of Beth is her inviting me back to her office to talk about disability studies. She didn't know it, but I'd already read her dissertation, some of her articles, and her book about children at-promise. I thought she was brilliant, and I was somewhat intimidated, so I avoided her classes that were heavy on theory, even though she'd asked me numerous times to join them. I'd already taken a few, but not any classes in the early childhood department. I was discouraged to engage with theory after taking a class with one notoriously difficult professor in another department.

Theory at the time felt like a bogus game of nonsensical academic jargon. I gave up on ever really thinking theory would be useful for me, especially after I'd tried in one paper (with that notoriously difficult professor) to use class structures as a metaphorical tool to look at ableism and audism, and how certain disabilities had more or less status based on visibility. The professor slammed the paper, and I hid.

And then one day, Beth bumped into me near the college of education offices. My good friend Bob and I were heading toward the stairs for lunch, when Beth came around the corner and spotted me. Beth was bubbling with her usual positive energy, and she said to me, "Joe, do you have some time? Come back to my office with me, I'd be really interested in hearing about what classes you want to take next semester."

Bob, knowing that I'd been worrying about Beth asking me to join those tough (and pointless, I felt) theory classes, walked off grinning, telling Beth as he rounded the stairs, "Oh, we were just going to go to lunch. But I've got some stuff to do first, so Joe, why don't you meet up with me when you're done."

I'm thinking Bob's going to get some payback later. I don't want to disappoint Beth because she seems so excited. So I go with her, thinking I'll stay for a little bit and hopefully stay strong enough not to let her convince me to take another theory course. After we talk some about my research interests, Beth is thrilled about the things I'm saying to her. She's interested in my background in literature and what I've learned about Deaf and disability studies over these years.

I'm a little bit taken aback by her saying that my life story could be used as research. She hands me a pile of books, dissertations, and articles that quickly start to stack up on the round table. I realize I have enough reading to keep me busy for some time. One of the books she hands me is on decolonizing methodologies in cross-cultural contexts, as well as a book on (dis)ability and semiotics. This is the beginning of my training in subaltern studies. She recommends I take some classes, but basically makes me promise to join her and Dr. Joseph Tobin in a publication seminar the following semester. Before the course begins, I stay up late many nights, reading all the materials Beth gave me.

I also read some of Dr. Tobin's work, becoming really excited by his evident interest in popular culture, which is also an interest of mine. By the next semester, I'd already read enough of both Drs. Swadener's and Tobin's work to feel unequivocally sure that they would figure out that I'd been tricking everyone all along in the doctoral program. They would find out what people back home already knew about me, that I was deaf and dumb.

One of the classes is meeting at a local coffee house, so I head over with Bob. I think to myself, I just need to hide so Drs. Swadener and Tobin don't talk with me. I stand near the couch area, waiting for everyone to get their coffees and sit down. Dr. Tobin comes through the door and I can feel nervousness dash down into my stomach. I'm the only one standing around, so Dr. Tobin approaches me after a quick hello to a few students by the cashier.

"Hi, Joe," He looks at me.

"Hi, Dr. Tobin," I answer, unsure what I'm going to talk with him about. I certainly don't want to bring up his work because then he'll know the truth about me. I'm itching to ask about the Pokémon book he edited. But I don't.

"Call me, Joe."

"Okey dokey, Joe," I say but it feels weird on my tongue.

We make some small talk, until he gets to my research interests.

I tell him, "I want to study something about deaf children."

He seems to become really interested, asking me, "What about deaf children do you want to study?"

"I don't know, maybe something with literacy and play," I say, reaching for a topic that is familiar to me as a classroom teacher. I'm looking around, hoping Bob will come over and save me. He sees me talking with Joe, smiles, and walks off.

Joe keeps talking with me, like I'm interesting, so now I'm getting nervous because I know the probability increases that I'm going to say something I regret, give away my dumbness. But instead I manage to say something in my nervousness that seems dismissive.

He tells me about his work on popular culture and media, and then asks me something about deaf children and popular culture, but I can't really hear what he's saying because all these people from our class are now piling into the small area we're talking in. I ask him to repeat what he said. He does, but I still can't hear what he's saying because now it's loud and I'm becoming increasingly more nervous. I realize I can't ask him, again, to repeat, so in a rush I say, "I'm not interested in popular culture."

What! My mind thinks to myself: Why did I just say that? Classmates moving a table and chairs around for our class meeting separate Joe and me. I feel I just lost my chance. He probably thinks I'm not interested in his work now. But I have no way to know what he thinks. I feel so disappointed.

But then the next time we meet, he invites me back to his office, and encourages me to take his course on educational ethnography the next fall, handing me summer readings on children and culture. During the semester, we work on over a dozen drafts of a dissertation proposal over the semester, and I'm starting to think about how I'm actually going to contribute to Deaf culture. I start to think about what I'm going to do to make sure children who have stories like and unlike my own get out to the general public, to those educating them in schools. Joe shares my aspiration that I write something that makes a difference; I learn we share a passion for provoking people to think, pushing the limits of what can be done. He gives me glimpses of how to use the Force, preparing me for what's to come.

I'm really excited that Joe keeps coming back to talk with me throughout the semester, he seems to find our conversations equally engaging. I can't understand why Beth and Joe want to talk with me. But these talks enliven me. It makes me start to wonder: Why are they treating my ideas like they're legitimate? Why do they keep referring to me as an authority on life growing up with deafness?

I start to seek out Beth whenever I go to campus, and she continues to give me more readings. I'd already spent years reading about Deaf culture, but now I'm learning about decolonizing strategies and tactics. She's getting me ready to use the Force.

The following fall, I'm in Joe's ethnography course. I realize that I'd been reading ethnographies, not knowing it as a genre, for years, beginning with Nora Ellen Groce's work on the historical Deaf community on Martha's Vineyard. This is the kind of writing that I've always loved reading, so I immerse myself in Joe's class. As time goes on, I start visiting with him even more frequently. One day we're in his office, talking about a final paper that is due for his course. I want to suggest the idea of using a short story as a vehicle to merge the ethnographic concepts we learned about in class with symbolic (re)representations of deafness in literature across time. I'm startled that Joe's so interested in the idea. What emerges is my Deaf version of H.G. Wells (2007) story "The Country of the Blind" titled, "Silent Civilization."

Joe shows me how to use my new superpowers of research and storytelling. He mentors me, and provokes me to think about how I could use my superpowers. It's not until I take Joe's post-structural theory course the following semester that I unlearn what I'd learned earlier about theory. We spend countless hours talking about methods and theoretical concepts I'm seeing that apply to my life. Joe, like me, sees theory as a tool (though I've always used the word metaphor); theory is not something we should believe in but something we should use. For someone who had grown up on the margins of society, I was suspicious of any overarching, grand narratives, critical of narratives that clearly marginalized difference. Joe encourages me to apply these theories we were learning to my own life, my past and present life. Discussions about my dissertation project on studying the enculturation of young children in preschools for the deaf led us both to travel down to Tucson to visit the Arizona State Schools for the Deaf and Blind.

On this trip I learn first hand how to conduct ethnographic fieldwork. He's teaching me how to harness the combined superpowers of research and storytelling, teaching me how to discover my counter life story, preparing me to document this journey ahead (that I had no inkling would be this way).

Beth gives me writing courage, sitting down with me at a computer, co-writing multiple reviews with me, I see how the mentor writes, how she wields her own superpowers with words that unmask the very feelings I could not earlier articulate without having learned about decolonizing ways of thinking and doing. She invites me to give class discussions on my topic. Doing this is intellectually and emotionally therapeutic; Beth gives me forums to talk my about my work, and over time I start to unlearn the oppression of my formative years from conversations with her, healing my body's memory.

As time goes on, I see myself changing; I see the subaltern Deaf superhero emerging as my mentors work with me, showing me how to wield my superpowers, releasing the superhero within me.

TWENTY-THREE

Super-Joe Takes Two Flights

FLIGHT ONE
Super-Joe Comes Out to Disability Studies

On Saturday, March 22, 2008, I fly from Phoenix Sky Harbor to John F. Kennedy airport in Queens, New York, arriving after ten at night. I look out the window, as the plane curves and starts to descend, watching the City lights twinkle magically to the backdrop of a dark night sky. I'm filled with anticipation, thinking about how my story first began thirty-two years ago on Long Island; how far I've come. I watch through the window, seeing Long Island appear toward the east where I grew up. I see the fish-shaped island's head protruding out from the City. I imagine the one hundred and eighteen miles of Long Island stretching narrowly toward the split of a fish's tail, where the north and south fork stretch out into the Atlantic beyond. The plane taxis, parks, and I make my way down the aisle, into the tunnel walkway toward the gate. While walking down the tunnel, I can feel my mind and body transforming, morphing with each step into my newly emerging subaltern superhero identity.

I see Jill, my sister, waiting by the gate for me. We hug and joke around some, and then make the necessary check-in phone call to Mom. Food is the main topic of discussion, but my mind is focused on the conference ahead. We head out to Long Island, to home. I spend the weekend with Jill, John, my brother, Nicole, his wife, Gabriella, my niece, my mom and Ernie, my step-father. I sit at the kitchen table at John's house and share some of the stories with them. They don't understand how I could be researching and writing about my own life story. For them, I'm Joey, not a Deaf subaltern superhero.

The day before my presentation, I take the Long Island Railroad out from the east end to the City, and then to save money I walk from Penn Station and up Park Avenue to meet with Joe Tobin at the apartment he's living in during his sabbatical leave from ASU. I'm excited to see Joe and my friends in what I feel to be my turf, New York. When I arrive, my two classmates from the doctoral programs at Arizona State University, Bob and Akiko, as well as Joe are waiting for me. We spend the rest of the day at the conference, arriving home after a late-night dinner. When we get back to Joe's place, everyone falls to sleep, exhausted from the day. I sit there, looking out the glass door, watching the City's night sky, taking in the emotions and thrills of coming home to present my first major conference paper on my life story. I'd presented at major conferences before. But this was personal. I feel unsure what my reception will be.

On Wednesday, March 26, I arrive at the room where the disability studies in education meeting will take place. The room is rectangular in shape. There are chairs about six or so rows back and twenty across. A raised platform for the presenters has a long table and chairs on it. I sit down at the presenter's table and shuffle some papers. People wander in and say hello to each other. I don't really know anyone by face, only names if I read their work.

I look at the faces of participants around me, some of whom are my favorite writers: Linda Ware, Philip Ferguson, Dianne Ferguson, Teri Holbrook, Jan Valle, and filmmaker Susan Hamovitch. Worry seeps into my stomach; I try to busy myself with shuffling my papers at the panelist table, try to not look like I'm counting the number of people in the room. I have to keep recounting because people keep moving around. We're about to begin, as Dr. Ware is signaling to everyone, so I pay attention to her as if I'm back in school, with my hands folded nicely on the table. I'm wondering if people see how nervous I am. Dr. Ware announces a few changes to the order of the program and we begin. I listen to the presentations before me, trying not to think about my own, but my worrying increases more as I wait my turn. Finally, Dr. Ware stands up and says something about my paper "d/Deaf and d/Dumb," I can't hear her because I'm feeling nervous, even as she is keeping in close proximity so I can see her face.

I get up to the podium, people are scrambling, trying to fix the PowerPoint so I can present, and I wave them off so they don't bother trying to get it to work. I don't need the PowerPoint to tell this story. I clear my throat, "Hi, everyone, if it looks like I'm nervous, it's because I am," the crowd of thirty-something people chuckle in unison, "I'm here today to tell you my story, this is my coming out as a Deaf and disability studies scholar and storyteller. I want you to sit back, close your eyes if you'd like, and imagine you're at a book reading...these are my stories..."

I read the vignettes about my birth and preschool years; I see people in the audience watching me. No one seems disinterested. After each vignette, I talk some about the weaving of multiple theories and the interviews with my informants. When I'm done I'm not too sure how I was received – what message did they get from my talk?

Philip Ferguson stands up to give his talk, but before he begins, he looks directly at me, "Joe, you belong here with us."

I start to beam, thinking about all those times I've sat rereading Dr. Ferguson's articles, admiring his writing flair and ways of critically examining disability constructions. He's one of my heroes.

Just after everyone presents, Dr. Ware discusses our papers. I want so badly to hear every word she has to say, I move in toward the table to listen as best as I can, and she starts by saying, "We as researchers need to start thinking about doing the kinds of things that Joe's done in his paper, the combination of theories and methods..." Her voice trails off. Dr. Ware's face looks like she really is saying something positive. I can hear her voice, but can't make out all the words. Her tone sounds like she's very excited.

I think to myself: Oh, no! She's saying all these things but I can't hear her! I want so badly to know what she's saying; my hearing aid pick up her voice again, "in combining the stories with..." Not again!

Everyone in the crowd is looking at me, as she talks, I read their faces. Their looks reassure me that everything is fine. Dr. Ware moves on to discuss another paper. Afterward everyone is in a rush to get out because another session is about to begin. But a number of people from the audience mill around waiting to talk with me. I'm surprised by the reception, scholars from all across the country asking me to see my work, to come and visit their universities to give talks, to join them at conferences. I feel like I do belong.

I walk up to Jan Valle just to say I admire her work, and that I hope to have a chance to collaborate with her in the future, she looks at me, and says, "We're going to adopt you!" We talk some more and Dr. Valle ends our conversations with words I'd been hoping to hear: "Your stories need to be told, Joe."

"Mine and many more."

FLIGHT TWO
Super-Joe Comes Out to Deaf Studies

On April 14, 2010, I fly from Tallahassee Regional Airport to Ronald Reagan Washington National Airport in Washington, D.C., landing just after sundown. Tomorrow Dr. Joseph Murray will lead an all-day seminar called "Difference as Diversity: Emerging Perspectives on Deaf-Gain, Disability, and Physical Diversity as an Enhancement of the Human Condition" hosted by Gallaudet University. Deaf studies and diversity scholars from within and outside the university will be presenting on the topic of Deaf-gain from multiple disciplinary angles.

I had been invited to give an afternoon talk on completed portions of d/Deaf and d/Dumb. When the Dean of Gallaudet, Carol Erting, who I'd been E-mailing with about another project, extended the offer to fly me out for the seminar as a guest speaker, I was thrilled. Carol's generosity and support of my work came at such a critical time. I was feeling inpatient that my road back to Gallaudet was taking too long and might never happen.

This opportunity to present on my work to, what was for me, a key audience was both exhilarating and scary. It was also a homecoming of sorts. I was going back to Gallaudet, where ten years earlier I met Dr. I. King Jordan and first made that promise to myself to contribute something to the Deaf-World. I saw this invited talk as one way to fulfill that promise.

I make my way through the airport quickly; there is not much of a crowd at this time, so I can speed walk easily. I hop on the Metro heading to Gallaudet University. As the train rides over a bridge, I look out the window as the historic sites to the northwest of the Potomac River roll on by: Jefferson Memorial, Lincoln Memorial, and the National Mall. At the New York Avenue–Florida Avenue–Gallaudet

University Metro station, I get off and walk about a little less than a mile to the university entrance. I stop at the gated entryway and take some pictures of the lit up Gallaudet University sign with my camera phone. I walk, exhausted with my luggage bag dragging behind me, to the Kellogg Conference Hotel located on the far side of the campus, where I'm staying for the next few days.

When I finally get into my hotel room, my body is ready to pass out. But my brain is on overdrive. I've been horribly nervous for days now. I didn't have an appetite these past days either. And, I hadn't slept too well on top of all that. In many ways, April 15 felt like Judgment Day for me.

I came to D.C. knowing that if the *d/Deaf and d/Dumb* book talk didn't go well, I would feel discouraged not only about finishing the writing of this book but also discouraged about whether I was really headed in the right direction on this journey to Deaf culture. There was so much riding on this trip.

I'm too worn-out to worry about tomorrow anymore and I fall into a deep sleep with my clothes and shoes still on.

On April 15, the sun rises at 6:23 a.m., I wake right after that. When my eyes blink open, my first thought is I get to meet some of my favorite writers at the seminar today. This makes me smile wide. I'm an unabashed academic groupie. Writers and intellectuals for me are like rock stars and million-dollar athletes (without the fame or money, of course).

I buy some coffee in a café by the lobby and make my way over to where the event will be held today. I'm early, so I walk the hallways and look at the names on each door. It's like walking past the shelves on my bookcase in my home office. As I turn one corner, I literally almost walk into Dr. Ben Bahan, a world-renowned ASL storyteller and Deaf studies scholar. He looks at me as if to see whether we might know one another but I look away because I'm afraid he will want to sign with me. I fear my sign skills are too weak and I won't make a good impression. Bahan walks in the opposite direction down the hall. I feel disappointed with the lost opportunity. I have a pep talk with myself in the hallway, finally resolving to try harder when I meet more people as the day goes on. ASL or no ASL, I'm going to be brave and meet people here for the seminar. I didn't want any more regrets.

As if on cue, my chance comes again.

Walking down the hall, I bump into the Deaf studies Dream-Team, Drs. Dirksen Bauman, M. J. Bienvenu, and Joseph Murray. I stay true to my promise and try to chat them up.

I make small talk with them using the little sign I do know, a good amount of gestures, and mostly finger spelling. I'm almost certain each of them wants to escape from this conversation because it takes me so long to say something simple in sign like, "Nice to meet you." I keep screwing up "meet you," positioning my hands in the wrong place because I'm nervous. But they are patient with me.

Not too long later, the interpreters show up. They shadow me everywhere I go for the rest of the day.

I notice Carol Erting come through the door so I approach her to say hello. She gives me a warm embrace, thanks me for coming, and I keep thanking her for inviting me – for giving me this chance to meet everyone here. Carol introduces me to other presenters and some faculty standing nearby. Everyone starts to settle into their seats for the seminar to kickoff so I sit down in the front row, with my hands folded in my lap, and watch the interpreter sitting right next to me. The interpreter transliterates and signs what is being said so I can read her lips and watch her hands.

The morning presentations go by quickly.

Lunch comes and goes. I'm having a blast as everybody mulls about before the afternoon seminar begins again. Slowly but surely, I come out of my shell and start to feel comfortable, chatting with everybody – the interpreters help me communicate not only with folks using ASL but also folks who speak. I've never been able to communicate with such ease. It's invigorating. For the first time in my life, I feel like I can understand everything that is being said. When I do miss something, the interpreters help. Having the interpreters was, to say the least, eye-opening.

After lunch, it is my turn to present.

I start off with reading the first chapter, "The Bottle Rocket Wars and Superhero Birthday," occasionally I look over to the interpreter to watch as she translates into ASL. I can see the entire audience of forty or fifty or so people, watching with intense interest. I can tell by their faces that the story and presentation is a hit.

I can now feel my mind and body transforming, morphing into my subaltern superhero identity.

A few minutes later, Ben Bahan comes up to me. I see this as my chance to make up for earlier when I avoided chatting with him. It's easy because now I have an interpreter.

Ben tells me about how he has been very interested in the term and idea of "deaf and dumb" too. He explains some of the history behind the use of the word that I didn't know. I'm so excited Ben is obviously interested in my work. So I decide to test out if this talk earned me enough capital to maybe get a meeting with Ben for tomorrow. When I ask, he quickly agrees for a meeting first thing in the morning.

After the day-long seminar ends, I pass out in the hotel room, watching the nightly news.

On April 16, for my 9 o'clock meeting, I meet Ben and the interpreter at his office. We hit it off chatting about the South Shore of Long Island, where he spent his summers as a child and I grew up. We both know the area and reminisce about old haunts, the Bay, the beach, and a place in Patchogue called Swan Bakery that makes the best jelly donuts.

Talking with Ben is like talking with a friend who also grew up in the same neighborhood. He feels so familiar.

Our time is almost up, I have to go to another meeting, so I try to squeeze in one more question before we have to go.

Through the interpreter, I ask Ben, "What advice would you give me to learn ASL? It's so hard because the ASL classes don't seem to work and I'm not around other Deaf people. I have such a hard time picking up ASL."

Ben says, "Come to my house."

I look at the interpreter and back to Ben.

"Repeat," I say to the interpreter.

She repeats, "Come to my house."

Ben can see I'm not sure what he's offering, so he explains, "The best way to learn ASL is through immersion, so come to my house, stay with me and my family. We're all Deaf."

"Are you serious," I ask.

"Yes," Ben says, wearing a face that teasingly reads – I dare you to come.

I respond with a smile, "Be careful what you offer, I will take you up on it."

"I'm serious. Come, stay at my home for a week or more, maybe even come a few times this summer. I'll teach you sign. I'll take you on a tour of Deaf culture too. You'll get a full immersion."

I look at Ben to see if he is one of those people who just say things but don't mean it. But he looks deadly serious.

I'm really touched by his sincerity.

We both have to go now because we're already late for another meeting. Even the interpreter points to her watch.

Before we go our separate ways, I say to Ben, "See you this summer then."

TWENTY-FOUR

Field Notes from Garcia's Mexican Restaurant

November 5, 2009 – PHOENIX, ARIZONA

After conducting a focus group with teachers and parents at the Phoenix School for the Deaf, our research team decides to go to Garcia's Mexican restaurant on 35th and Peoria for dinner. PJ and Scott are both teachers at the school for the deaf and are Deaf themselves; Jennifer, hearing herself, is a child of a deaf adult (CODA), and interprets for the project; Tommy, who is Deaf too, is partnering with Joe Tobin and me on this comparative, ethnographic study of kindergartens in schools for the deaf.

All of us settle around a rectangular-shaped table. Jennifer positions herself at the end of table so she can interpret for all of us. PJ, Scott, and Tommy chat in ASL, while Jennifer translates what they say into English for Joe and me. When Joe and I talk, Jennifer translates what we say into ASL for PJ, Scott, and Tommy. The conversation flows remarkably well between the two languages. Jennifer doesn't seem overwhelmed by the task of interpreting for all five of us.

We chat about our project for a while. Then the conversation turns to me:

Tommy: Joe (Valente), why did you tell everyone today that you're deaf?
Me: Well, I want them to know that I'm Deaf like them. I want them to know who I am.
Tommy: I understand that you want them to know that this project is both personal and professional, but it seems a bit odd that you tell people you're Deaf.
Me: Why?
Tommy: Because, if you're black – do you tell someone when you meet, "Hi, I'm black?"

Everybody around the table laughs. I do too.

Me: I want people to know that I'm proud Deaf, that I'm not hard-of-hearing – I hate when people say that.
Tommy: People will know that you're Deaf, Joe (Valente), because you sign, so there's no reason to declare that you're Deaf. Deaf people know other people are Deaf people because they share the same language.
PJ: Yes, when I traveled to Europe, and I'd meet someone who is Deaf – immediately, we can communicate – like, when I was in Italy, I met some Deaf Italians – quickly I picked it up and when I came back to the US, I was back in the classroom and kept forgetting that I was using ISL, not ASL...

PJ acts out a scene where he smacks his hand to show he keeps accidently slipping into ISL, instead of ASL. His face shows confusion, even pulls his left and right hands closer to his face to examine them, as if they are working independently of him. Everybody watches PJ perform. He's good, really good.

PJ: ...even when I'm in the airport, I'm always looking around to see if anyone is signing...

PJ lifts his head, motions to look around the restaurant, as if he's in an airport, his face looks one way, then another. Finally he spots the imaginary Deaf person in the airport, he smiles, nods his head at this imaginary person, and mimics running over to say salute (hello).

Tommy: Yeah, Deaf people know you're Deaf because you sign; they use their eyes – you need to learn to sign, Joe (Valente)!

Me: I'm trying! I've been learning ASL for years but it's never enough. I'm alone. Don't have anyone to sign with. It's not easy. Like, tonight during the focus group. It was so frustrating. Here I am watching all the focus group informants signing and the interpreters speaking aloud, and yet I'm missing everything. Ugh! I can't understand all the signs clearly. And, I can't read the lips of the interpreters! The interpreters were standing behind me, so I missed so much!

PJ: Why didn't you ask for interpreters for yourself?

Joe: Why didn't you say something?

Tommy: You say you're...

Tommy pumps his chest with his fist, covers one ear and throws out a Deaf power salute.

Tommy: ...you say you're proud Deaf. You say you're Deaf, but you act like a hearing person who can't hear. I don't think you've come to terms with being Deaf. You still think you're hearing. If you did think you were Deaf, you would ask for everyone to accommodate you. But you don't. Instead you accept missing so much.

Me: I don't know why I didn't say anything. I guess I'm so used to missing so much, I just don't think about it. I'm really upset with myself for not saying something. I wish I knew sign!

Joe: I keep asking you this, but there must be a reason why you've still not learned sign. You're intelligent, so there's no reason why you can't or couldn't have done this already. What I don't understand is why you've not done it yet. Are you afraid?

Me: Afraid of what?

Joe: Well, in order to gain something, you have to lose something. If you sign, you have to accept that you're not going to be able to communicate as eloquently as you can with speech, at least until you become fluent in sign, which will take a while, and even then you might not be as good a communicator as you are now in English. I don't know if you all know this...

Joe looks around the table.

> Joe: ...but Joe (Valente) is really eloquent, he's a great speaker – he's gifted in the way he talks. Joe (Valente), if you sign, then you're no longer eloquent. If you sign, then you lose the ability to communicate as beautifully as you do – you're the equivalent of a child learning a language with ASL. You may be saying something in sign, using the very little sign you know, and be thinking, "Well, if I said this in English, I could be more clear, I could be more eloquent." That means you have to give up what is your strength – communicating. That's a risk.

No one says anything for a while. Everyone eats for a little bit until PJ finally says something in sign for Jennifer to translate. PJ wears a determined look on his face.

> PJ: I want to get back to what I asked you before, Why didn't you ask for interpreters? Do you have interpreters at Florida State yet?
> Me: No.
> PJ: Why not?
> Me: Because, well, I really don't know.
> PJ: Joe (Valente), I see it in your eyes. You pretend you are following along, but I know when you are lost. You were lost many times during the focus group. I saw you get lost a lot.
> Tommy: Yes, I did notice too. You pretend to understand.
> Joe: Whew! This is like an intervention.

Everyone around the table laughs. The mood lightens noticeably.

> PJ: I'm sorry I put you on the hot-seat.
> Me: It's fine. When I get to Florida State, I'm going to go back to taking ASL classes again and get interpreters, I think.
> PJ: Will you really?
> Me: I'm thinking I just might.

TWENTY-FIVE

Going Native at Ben Bahan's House

It's 4:00 a.m. on Friday, June 25, 2010, I wake up with anticipation and nervousness for the day ahead. I go to reach for my hearing aid in the side drawer, only to realize for today – well, for the next week really – I won't need it. Not for the journey ahead. I'm flying from Tallahassee, Florida, to Baltimore-Washington International (BWI) Airport, where Dr. Ben Bahan will pick me up. I'm going native at Ben Bahan's house.

Ben likes to joke that everyone in his family is Deaf, except the dog.

I won't need my hearing aid because there will be no speaking, only sign for the coming week. It's total immersion. Ben offered to be both my host and guide on this journey into one corner of the DEAF-WORLD, located in Frederick, Maryland, where he, family, and close friends reside.

I can feel the tension and thrill seep down my spine as I step from the bed. Allison, my fiancé, is already one step ahead of me, as she is every morning. Alli already has a cup of coffee in hand for me before I can get into the hallway. I can see she is excited and nervous too.

I take a sip from my coffee. It's the part of the morning I cherish most, so I take my time and don't rush. I look into our bedroom. Except for the bed, it's empty. There are boxes everywhere throughout the house. We're in the process of packing up and leaving Florida for good in four weeks. I just recently accepted an offer to go work for Pennsylvania State University. We're excited to be closer to our families in Ohio and Long Island.

Our dogs, Scout – a Border collie, healer mix – and Beau – a Labrador mix – know something is up. They get clingy when the suitcase comes out of the closet. I drink coffee and stare into space; Alli scurries about with edgy energy; I watch Scout and Beau wrestle on the bed, wonder if I need to shave, rubbing my cheeks. Is this a business trip? Or is it personal? That's my usual barometer if I'm going to have to shave.

I elect not to shave.

Alli does the usual check-down to see that I have everything I need for the trip ahead. She tells me, "I'm so proud of you. You're going to have such a fun time with Ben. You're going to learn so much."

"I hope I can pick up sign fast," I tell her. She already knows I'm worried that I'm too slow a learner. We've been chatting about this for weeks now.

"You'll do fine, Joe."

Beau and Scout manage to get tangled enough in their wrestling match to fall off the bed onto the floor. Quickly they get back into the wrestling ring that is our bed. I stuff some random clothes into the bag, even a nice dress shirt.

I shower quickly and grab the bag to leave. Alli already has the 4Runner running in the garage, the dogs in the back seat, ready to go.

I get into the driver's seat. Alli taps my arm. I read her lips, she asks, "Do you have your hearing aid?"

"No," I say, "I won't need it, hon. Everyone's Deaf."

"I know. But what about the airport and other places?"

I know she's worried that I'll regret not having it with me just in case but I get terse, "Don't worry about it. It'll be fine."

For this trip, I'm going total immersion. No hearing aid.

"Okay," Alli tells me, but her face doesn't look too sure.

"It'll be like when I was in high school and I threw out the hearing aid, Alli. It'll be like those days."

"Whatever you want to do," she lips, "let's get going or you're going to be late."

We get on the road and make it to the Tallahassee Regional Airport with plenty of time to spare. I pull up to the curb and Alli turns to me, "I love you. You're going to have a wonderful time. Text me when you get there. I can't wait for you to tell me what happens."

We kiss. She gets out of the truck to take the keys from me to drive home, gives me one last hug.

I say my good-byes to Alli, Scout, and Beau – my family. Every time I leave them for a trip, I feel sad and get sentimental. I watch the 4Runner pull away from the curb before I turn to walk through the automatic doors into the airport. I look around the lobby; it's there that I realize I've now entered a new world. Not everyone is going to understand how to talk with me like Alli does; she knows how to communicate with and without the hearing aid in.

I briskly walk the length of the long corridor toward the security checkpoint, pulling the suitcase on its wheels from behind. I'm a pro at traveling – tickets and license are already in hand by the time I get to the security counter, where the TSA agent waits.

When I approach the agent, I don't say anything. I sign, "Hello."

The TSA agent catches on real quick. He mimics my motion back, "Hello."

I hand him my tickets and license. He attempts small talk in gestures. The TSA agent mimes a, 'it's nice outside, yes?' I nod in the affirmative. The agent then lips, "Have a nice trip."

I give an emphatic, "Thank you," in sign.

After I pass through the metal detector, another TSA agent comes over to me. I can read his lips say something about having to recheck the computer bag. He pulls a book from my bag, motions to show me that it's obstructing the x-ray's vision.

I sign, "Hello, Deaf."

The agent gestures that he's going to put the computer bag through the x-ray machine one more time. He hands me the book to hold. His gestures are methodical and clear.

I'm impressed.

It seems so odd. With my hearing aid in, most of the time people lose their patience and get annoyed when they are forced to repeat what they've said. Usually people raise their voices, but now with gestures and sign, these people are much more patient and better communicators. I start to think I might do this more often when I travel.

I get on the small wing-propeller Atlantic Southeast Airlines plane; they do the local connections for Delta Air Lines to their hub in Atlanta. I sit in my usual window seat in the very back right across from the bathroom and open up the book I brought along for the trip. It's an old beat-up copy of *A Journey into the Deaf-World* by Harlan Lane, Robert Hoffmeister, and Ben Bahan.

I notice the flight attendant keeps looking at the book and me. Back and forth. It looks like he's wondering if I'm Deaf.

I gesture to ask if he has a pen.

He hands one to me as the plane taxis down the runway. Just before takeoff, the flight attendant comes over to me and fingerspells what I realize to be his name. He smiles before sitting down. I smile back.

Once the plane tilts up and into the sky, I have a brief panic that I lost my hearing aid. I feel foolish. How quickly do I forget I left it at home on purpose?

I read *A Journey into the Deaf-World* for a few minutes until the Captain's voice comes blaring through the speakers. I'm shocked to hear his voice. I thought for sure without the hearing aid on, I wouldn't hear anything. Without the aid on, I can't hear the human voice very much. But for some odd reason, I can hear voices better on phones or loudspeakers. Anyway, when the Captain's voice comes through, I'm surprised. I try to listen to what it is that he's saying. But I can't make out the words. His sounds are garbled. I catch a few words here and there, something about arriving to Atlanta later than planned because of some wind or some such thing. I really don't know.

Since I can't hear what it is that he's saying, I try to go back to reading my book. But I can't because the loudspeaker is blaring garbled sounds into my ear and it keeps distracting me.

I really start to get pissed because I can't concentrate.

The best part of being deaf is how it helps me stay focused for long periods of time without distractions.

But this Captain's long and loud monologue keeps going on and on. Just when I think he's finished, he starts up all over again. This goes on for about ten or so minutes, much to my and, I start to see, other passengers' annoyance. Some of them start to look at the flight attendant, as if to say, "Tell the Captain to shut-up."

The flight attendant actually looks like he's going to go do this but then the pilot goes quiet.

I go back to reading.

Throughout the rest of the flight, every time the talkative pilot gets on the loudspeaker, I get madder and madder. Not so much at him for not shutting up. But because this all reminds me that I can "hear" even though I can't make the words out too well. It's a reminder I'm in-between two worlds, even without the hearing aid on. I can't make the world go totally silent.

Finally we arrive at Atlanta to change airplanes; there is only a ten-minute layover so I have to hustle to the train to get to the next terminal for the already boarded plane to BWI Airport. As soon as I get onto the Delta Air Lines Boeing 737-700, we taxi and take off in minutes. This pilot doesn't say much beyond a few terse words. I'm relieved and dive into my book. We arrive at BWI shortly thereafter and I make my way off the plane. When I step into the airport, it's as if I'm entering a new country. I'm like one of those naïve and pesky travelers, too overwhelmed by the sights and smells to move around with any efficiency. It doesn't feel like I'm still in the United States; certainly doesn't feel like I'm just outside Baltimore. My imagination helps to trick my conscious mind to play the part of an anthropologist going native in some faraway locale.

Without my hearing aid on, I notice I rely on my eyes even more. I already consider myself a person of the eye but now more so than ever before. My other senses go into overdrive too.

I feel a vibration from my cell phone. It's Ben. He texts to tell me to meet at the arrival/pickup area outside. I text back that I'm here and heading his way.

I can smell and taste crab cakes frying on a grill in the airport café near the gate, I'm tempted to stop in when I pass the black chalkboard sign that reads: Maryland Crab Cake Sandwich with French Fries, Cole Slaw, Biscuit, and Coca Cola for $4.99. It takes all my self-control not to stop in there for a quick bite.

When I finally get outside, I start looking around for Ben's truck. I can't see him. I keep looking and looking. He texts me again to see if I'm there yet. I text him back and tell him I'm already here, looking for him.

After a few minutes pass, I realize I'm standing at the curb of the departure area. But there is no sign to the arrival zone so I'm confused. I don't want to text Ben that I got all mixed up so I look for someone official-looking.

I spot a guy in a red coat and cap. I go to ask for directions but since this is full immersion, I won't use my voice. I approach the man, gesturing and using the little sign I do know to tell him I'm trying to find the arrival area. After repeated attempts to get him to understand, he still doesn't get what I'm asking.

Finally an idea comes to me. I take out my phone and show him the texts from Ben that explains where to meet him. Redcoat nods his head up-and-down that he gets it and points me back into the airport to a set of stairs leading downward to another level below.

I thank him and walk really fast with my bag rolling in tow. When I come out to the curb where the arrival zone is, I can see Ben parked in his blue Toyota Sequoia. Our eyes lock. We wave to one another across a long distance. I get to Ben's truck, throw my luggage into the backseat, and jump up into the passenger seat. We shake hands. I look at Ben, smiling and wondering: How in the world are we going to communicate during the one hour ride to his house in rural Maryland?

Ben drives off. We start with some gestures and sign. He's using simple words in ASL that he knows I already know, which are not too many. It feels like we're testing one another out to see how we're going to do this – it's a preview of the week ahead. No English, only ASL and gestures.

As he drives and looks at me to communicate, he has to repeat himself because I have a hard time understanding at first. I'm anxious and can't focus too well. I worry about him not keeping his eyes entirely and solely on the road ahead. Then as I watch him, I learn he brings new meaning to having eyes on the back of one's head. Ben can see 360 degrees, signing to me, watching my response in a mix of sign and gestures, all the while masterfully steering us through Baltimore traffic exiting and dispersing into suburbia.

We chat about etymology. I love etymology. Ever since I was a kid, I was fixated on word origins. As we drive, I learn Ben shares this hobby too. I keep asking him to explain the origin of words he shows me that I don't know. After a while, I'm certain Ben must be either annoyed or hopelessly bored with my incessant questions. But every time I look at his face for clues, he just wears a sort of goofy smile, like this whole experience tickles him. I later learn this is just how Ben is no matter what. Life tickles him.

I'm thankful he gives explanations of each word; sometimes he doesn't know the word origin so he guesses by acting out some silly scene. When I was learning English vocabulary words as a middle schooler, I used to study word origins because it seemed to help the definition stick in my head. If a word had an interesting background story, it made it easier to remember. Ben's word charades help.

We chat about a slew of topics in quick succession: Ben's long commute to DC on the train everyday; an accident we pass where a van was on fire; how many classes we each teach a semester; about his kids, Davy and Juliana, and his wife, Sue, as well as all the people we're going to meet on this tour of the DEAF-WORLD over the next week; how Frederick is a "Deaf town" where even local shopkeepers know sign; his iPhone that comes in next week; about his friend, Bob, who we're going to meet for lunch right now and a different Bob we're going to meet the last days I'm here to visit.

After Ben gives me some background on the second Bob, I finally realize this other Bob I'm going to meet is the Robert Hoffmeister "Bob" from *A Journey into the Deaf-World*. He was co-author with Ben (and Harlan Lane) on the book I've been re-reading for this trip. It seems that the three of us are going boating or sailing in the Chesapeake later in the week. There's really no time to digest any of this or worry too much about whether I'm using ASL words correctly or if my gesturing makes any sense.

As we head into the town of Frederick, Maryland, with its mix of Colonial and Civil War era buildings and stately red-brick houses, we pull around one corner onto a Main Street. It's a shopping district with picturesque store-front windows and crowds milling about with no sense of urgency. The pace here may be slower but I'm feeling a bit overwhelmed by all this – the adrenaline kick that got me through most of the day so far starts to wear off.

I watch the store fronts as we drive on by: antique stores, brew pubs, coffee shops, a tavern and grill, a bed and breakfast, even a tea room. Frederick looks cozy and charming. The slow ride makes me feel a little sleepy.

We slowly drive our way through a bit of a traffic jam and turn off to a two-lane side street, Ben explains we have one more thing to do before we go meet his friend, Bob, for lunch downtown at a fancy place called Volt. We need to pick up his son, Davy, from basketball camp and take him to a family friend, whose son is about the same age.

As we make our way into an expansive school campus, I can make out the sign that reads: Maryland School for the Deaf.

I'm excited to see what the school grounds look like. Whenever I visit a school for the deaf on research projects, I like to walk around and learn about the buildings and the history. As if he's reading my mind, Ben leans over to explain that I'm going on a tour of the school later in the week with the superintendent, Jamie, who is also a long-time family friend of his. Jamie is coming over to Ben's house later tonight.

When we pick up Davy at the basketball courts, we play a few rounds of half-court basketball with Davy's friend and his father. A few minutes go by and a gym teacher-looking man comes into the gymnasium. To everyone we meet, Ben explains why I'm here. Everyone says some variation of "welcome" and something with the word "journey." It's as if I'm a fellow traveler, going to a place they already know.

We meet up with Ben's friend at Volt for beers. After two drinks, we head to Ben's house for coffee and snacks. We sit on the porch. Bob leaves and some local kids come by looking for Davy and Juliana. Neither of the kids is home. Davy is still at his friend's house. I finally realize Juliana is with her mother, Sue, visiting grandparents in Boston for the weekend. Somehow I missed Ben tell me about this earlier. He chats with me as if he already did. I then remember he told me about it in an E-mail before I came.

I start to yawn a lot and to get really tired, especially since I'm not used to getting up at 4 a.m. and meeting so many new people, but I don't want to crash just yet. Davy comes back and his friend's family comes too. Everybody just sits on the porch and signs with one another. For the most part, I think I can follow what is being said when the conversation is simple. Davy and his friends sign with me about football. They're patient with me as I struggle to find the words in sign to say what I want to say.

A little later, Jamie, the superintendent of the Maryland School for the Deaf, comes over as well. We all chat about the school, football, and how amazing the fireworks are for the Fourth of July.

When the neighborhood kids and their mom go home, Davy goes inside the house, and it's just Ben, Jamie, and me sitting on the porch. It's a quiet night, only occasionally does a car drive by the house. We sit there, no one's signing. Everyone is deep in thought.

I can't help but to sit there and think about today. I soak it all in — from leaving Alli and the dogs this morning, the flight from Florida to Maryland, seeing the school for the deaf, meeting all these Deaf folks, and now just sitting here on the porch. Everything seems so still compared to earlier in the day. I start to wish really badly that I lived in Frederick and could hang out with Ben's amazing circle of friends and neighbors.

After some quiet time, somehow Ben, Jamie, and I get to chatting about school and work. Jamie looks over to me, using sign and when I don't understand, speech too, he says, "Do you have interpreters at your job?"

"No," I say.

"Why?" Jamie's face looks surprised.

"I'm *not* disabled," I sign as best I can, emphasizing the *not* with an attempt at dramatic flair.

I continue: "I" – since I don't know the ASL word for "refuse," I substitute it in English, then go back to ASL for the rest – "to say I'm disabled!"

Ben, sitting in the rocker at the edge of the porch, watches this exchange between Jamie and me. He looks partly entertained and uncertain where all this will lead. Jamie is clearly pissed that I don't have interpreters, he goes on, "Why?"

I explain in a mix of English, finger-spelling, sign, and gestures, "My two Deaf friends, PJ and Tommy, both already talked to me about this. They said I needed to get interpreters. I tried to at Florida State. But I refuse to say I'm disabled because I'm not, I'm Deaf."

Jamie looks confused, "What do you mean?"

This is where I break the no-speaking rule repeatedly. I keep catching myself slipping back into English. I feel bad because I told Ben I would not speak, only sign. But I can't stop. And, Ben doesn't stop me.

"At Florida State, I had to fill out this form for the ADA office to get interpreters. The form wanted me to write about my disability and how my disability prevents me from performing my duties. I refuse to say I'm disabled. I'm Deaf," I go on for a long time more about why this is not just political or cultural but because this is how my mom raised me – I don't have a disability. I won't become disabled now, not after holding out this long. Being Deaf means I belong to a culture, not a disability category. I can't explain any of this to Jamie and Ben effectively so I don't.

I do tell them about the part that pissed me off the most about those ADA forms, "Those forms, they wanted me to tell them how I can't perform my job duties. I told them, I *can* perform my job duties. It's just that everyone at Florida State *can't* communicate with me effectively, that's the disability," I'm not sure how much of this they are getting because I'm bouncing between sign, gestures, and ASL but I vent more, "the dumb form wanted me to tell them moments when my disabling condition prevented me from doing my job – like I'm supposed to write down incidents where I didn't hear – how would I know what I didn't hear? What a dumb form."

Jamie's face still looks incredulous. I think he's not getting what it is I'm saying. He says, "Fine. Fine! You are not disabled. What does it matter? You are Deaf. Who cares? The government doesn't care about the difference between disabled and Deaf. It's just words. You need the interpreter. What do you do in meetings?"

I shrug my shoulders, "I do like I always did in school, I daydream."

Jamie's face goes bright red. He lifts himself forward some in the chair, readies himself to say something.

"Oh, no. Here comes the Jamie treatment," I can see Ben laughs some to himself, he folds his arms to watch, as if he's seen Jamie perform this intervention before.

I watch Jamie carefully; his face shows not so much anger but exasperation. I start to wonder if I'm being stubborn. I wonder if I need to think some more about this. I'm still uncertain.

All doubt disappears once Jamie says these words both loudly orally and in ASL, "When you do that, you hurt me! You hurt Ben! You hurt many of us!"

Ben's face shows shock. I can see he's about to intercede and tell Jamie to layoff some.

My heart sinks. It dawns on me how right he is. I never thought about it that way.

I say, "I'm sorry. I didn't think of it that way. I just thought I was only hurting me. I'm just so used to not understanding what is going on around me."

Jamie softens some, I'm guessing even he is surprised by his own outburst, "You are a smart guy. You have so much to offer," he pokes the air hard with his finger to emphasize the "You-s" when signing, "You have so much to bring to the department, wherever you are, you can't help that you can't hear your colleagues or that they don't know sign."

Ben finally breaks his silence and chimes in, "The interpreter is not for you, but for others." This reminds me of the saying that hearing folks are sign-impaired, not that Deaf people are hearing-impaired. I laugh some to myself, imagining myself telling my new colleagues at Pennsylvania State University that they are sign-impaired.

Jamie adds to Ben's comment, "The interpreter is for ALL of us."

Everything goes quiet. Each of us is exhausted so we just rock in our chairs on the porch for a good amount of time. I'm lost in thought, thinking about what I'm going to do differently when I go to Penn State. For sure, I'm going to get interpreters now.

Not too long later, Jamie leaves, and we all go to bed. I can't believe that this is just my first night here. There is still a week more to go. Just before I nod off, I think to myself:

It's not so much that I've managed to find success in the larger, hearing world or that I've finally found Deaf culture. What I'm learning from this journey is how to more fully start living in both places.

REFERENCES

Althusser, L. (1972). *Lenin and philosophy, and other essays*. New York: Monthly Review Press.

Apple, M. W. (1990). *Ideology and curriculum*. Routledge Education Books. London: Routledge & K. Paul.

Baker, B. (2002). The hunt for disability: The new eugenics and the normalization of school children. *Teachers College Record, 104*(4), 663–703.

Baker, B. (2003). Hear Ye! Hear Ye! Language, deaf education, and the governance of the child in historical perspective. In M. N. Bloch, *Governing children, families, and education: Restructuring the welfare state* (pp. 287–312). New York: Palgrave Macmillan.

Barone, T. (2001). *Touching eternity: The enduring outcomes of teaching*. New York: Teachers College Press.

Bauman, H. -D. L. (2004). Audism: Exploring the metaphysics of oppression. *Journal of Deaf Studies and Deaf Education. 9*(2), 239–246.

Baynton, D. C. (1996). *Forbidden signs: American culture and the campaign against sign language*. Chicago: University of Chicago Press.

Bertling, T. (1994). *A child sacrificed: To the deaf culture*. Wilsonville, OR: Kodiak Media Group.

Bowker, G. & Star, S. (2002). *Sorting things out: Classification and its consequences*. Cambridge, MA: MIT Press.

Breivik, J-K. (2005). *Deaf identities in the making: Local lives transnational connections*. Washington, DC: Gallaudet University Press.

Brueggemann, B. J. (1999). *Lend me your ear: Rhetorical constructions of deafness*. Washington, DC: Gallaudet University Press.

Brueggemann, B. J. (2004). *Literacy and deaf people: Cultural and contextual perspectives*. Washington, DC: Gallaudet University Press.

Bruner, J. S. (1990). *Acts of meaning*. The Jerusalem-Harvard lectures. Cambridge, MA: Harvard University Press.

Butler, J. (1999). *Gender trouble: Feminism and the subversion of identity*. New York: Routledge.

Clandinin, D. J., & Connelly, F. M. (2000). *Narrative inquiry: Experience and story in qualitative research*. San Francisco: Jossey-Bass.

Cornelius, J. (1983). "We sipped and learned to read": Slave accounts of the literacy process. *Phylon, 44*(3), 171–186.

D'Andrade, R. G. (1995). *The development of cognitive anthropology*. Cambridge: Cambridge University Press.

Danforth, S., Slocum, L., & Dunkle, J. (2010). Turning the educability narrative: Samuel Kirk at the intersection of learning disability and "mental retardation." *Journal of Intellectual and Developmental Disabilities, 48*(3), 180–194.

Danforth, S., Taff, S., & Ferguson, P. (2006). Place, profession, and program in the history of special education curriculum. In E. A. Brantlinger, *Who benefits from special education?: Remediating (fixing) other people's children*. Studies in curriculum theory. Mahwah, NJ: L. Erlbaum Associates.

Delgado, R., & Stefancic, J. (2001). *Critical race theory: An introduction*. Critical America. New York: New York University Press.

Del Valle, S. (2003). *Language rights and the law in the United States: Finding our voices*. Tonawanda, NY: Multilingual Matters Ltd.

Duranti, A. (1997). *Linguistic anthropology*. Cambridge: Cambridge University Press.

Eisenhart, M. (2001). Educational ethnography past, present, and future: Ideas to think with. *Educational Researcher, 30*(8), 16–27.

Eisner, E. W. (1991). *The enlightened eye: Qualitative inquiry and the enhancement of educational practice*. New York: Macmillan.

Erickson, F. (2004). *Talk and social theory: Ecologies of speaking and listening in everyday life*. Cambridge: Polity Press.

Foucault, M. (1978). *The history of sexuality*. New York: Pantheon Books.

Foucault, M. (1992). The subject and power. In D. Ingram, J. Simon-Ingram, & D. Ingram, *Critical theory: The essential readings*. Paragon issues in philosophy. New York: Paragon House.

Foucault, M. (1995). *Discipline and punish: The birth of the prison*. New York: Pantheon Books.

Freire, P. (1985). *Pedagogy of the oppressed*. Pelican books. Harmondsworth, Middlesex: Penguin.

Gramsci, A., Hoare, Q., & Nowell-Smith, G. (2005). *Selections from the prison notebooks of Antonio Gramsci*. New York: International.

Gundaker, G. (1998). *Signs of diaspora / diaspora of signs: Literacies, creolization, and vernacular practice in African America*. The Commonwealth Center Studies in American culture. New York: Oxford University Press.

Gundaker, G. (2007). Hidden education among African Americans during slavery. *Teachers College Record, 109*(7), 1591–1612.

Hole, R. D. (2004). *Narratives of identity: A poststructural analysis of three deaf women's life stories*. (Ph.D. Thesis). University of British Columbia, Vancouver, BC.

Holland, D. & Lave, J. (2001). History in person: An introduction. In D. Holland & J. Lave (Eds.), *History in person: Enduring struggles, contentious practice, intimate identities* (pp. 3–33). Santa Fe, NM: School of American Research Press.

Humphries, T. (1975). *Audism: The birth of a word*. Unpublished essay.

Jankowski, K. A. (1997). *Deaf empowerment: Emergence, struggle, and rhetoric*. Washington, DC: Gallaudet University Press.

Joyce, J. (1939). *Finnegans wake*. New York: Viking Press.

Kaomea, J. (2003). Reading erasures and making the familiar strange: Defamiliarizing methods for research in formerly colonized and historically oppressed communities. *Educational Researcher, 32*(2), 14–25.

Kaomea, J. (2004). Dilemmas of an indigenous academic: A native Hawaiian story. In K. Mutua, & B. B. Swadener, *Decolonizing research in cross-cultural contexts: Critical personal narratives*. Albany, NY: State University of New York Press.

Kaomea, J. (2005). Indigenous studies in the elementary curriculum: A cautionary Hawaiian example. *Anthropology and Education Quarterly, 36*(1), 24–42.

Klock, G. (2002). *How to read superhero comics and why.* New York: Continuum.

Kuppers, P. (2006). Blindness and affect: Daredevil's site/sight. *Quarterly Review of Film and Video, 23*(2), 89–96.

Ladd, P. (2003). *Understanding deaf culture in search of deafhood.* Clevedon, England: Multilingual Matters.

Ladd, P. (2005). Deafhood: A concept stressing possibilities, not deficits. *Scandinavian Journal of Public Health, 33*(Supplement), 12–17.

Ladson-Billings, G., & Tate, W. F. (2006). *Education research in the public interest: Social justice, action, and policy.* New York: Teachers College Press.

Lane, H. L. (2002). Do deaf people have a disability? *Sign Language Studies, 2*(4), 356–379.

Lane, H. (2005). Ethnicity, ethics, and the deaf-world. *Journal of Deaf Studies and Deaf Education, 10*(3), 291–320.

Lincoln, Y. S., & Guba, E. G. (1985). *Naturalistic inquiry.* Beverly Hills, CA: Sage Publications.

Linton, S. (1998). *Claiming disability knowledge and identity.* New York: New York University Press.

Loomba, A. (1998). *Colonialism-postcolonialism.* The new critical idiom. London: Routledge.

Luttrell, W. (2005). "Good enough" methods for life-story analysis. In N. Quinn, *Finding culture in talk: A collection of methods.* Culture, mind, and society. New York: Palgrave Macmillan.

Mattingly, C., & Garro, L. C. (2000). *Narrative and the cultural construction of illness and healing.* Berkeley: University of California Press.

McCarty, T. L. (2005). *Language, literacy, and power in schooling.* Mahwah, NJ: L. Erlbaum Associates.

McDermott, R. & Raley, J. D. (2007). From John Dewey to an anthropology of education. *Teachers College Record, 109*(7), 1820–1835.

McDougall, K. (2007).'Ag-shame' and superheros: Stereotype and the signification of disability. In B. Watermeyer, *Disability and social change: A South African agenda.* Cape Town, South Africa: HSRC Press.

Mehan, H. (1993). Beneath the skin and between the ears. In S. Chaiklin & J. Lave (Eds.), *Understanding practice* (pp. 241–269). New York: Cambridge University Press.

Mitchell, D. D. (2006). Flashcard: Alternating between visible and invisible identities. *Equity & Excellence in Education, 39*, 137–145.

Mitchell, D. T., & Snyder, S. L. (2000). *Narrative prosthesis: Disability and the dependencies of discourse.* Corporealities. Ann Arbor: University of Michigan Press.

Mutua, K., & Swadener, B. B. (2004). *Decolonizing research in cross-cultural contexts: Critical personal narratives.* Albany, NY: State University of New York Press.

Nasir, N.S. & Hand, V.M. (2006). Exploring sociocultural perspectives on race, culture, and learning. *Review of Educational Research,* 76(4), 449–475.

Ochs, E., & Capps, L. (2001). *Living narrative: Creating lives in everyday storytelling.* Cambridge, MA: Harvard University Press.

Padden, C., & Humphries, T. (2005). *Inside deaf culture.* Cambridge, MA: Harvard University Press.

Phillipson, R. (2000). English as an exclusionary language. In M. Reisigl & R. Wodak, *The semiotics of racism: Approaches in critical discourse analysis.* Wien: Passagen.

Reeve, D. (2002). Negotiating psycho-emotional dimensions of disability and their influence on identity constructions. *Disability and Society, 17*(5), 493–508.

Rockwell, E. (2005). Indigenous accounts of dealing with writing. In T. McCarty (Ed.), *Language, literacy and power in schooling* (pp. 5–27). Mahwah, NJ: LEA.

Rolfe, S. & MacNaughton, G. (2001). "Research as a tool." In S. Rolfe, G. MacNaughton, & I. Siraj-Blatchford (Eds.), *Doing early childhood research: Theory and practice* (pp. 3–11). Buckingham: Open University Press.

Said, E. W. (1978). *Orientalism*. New York: Pantheon Books.

Said, E. W. (1993). *Culture and imperialism*. London: Chatto & Windus.

Senghas, R. J., & Monaghan, L. (2002). Signs of their times: Deaf communities and the culture of language. *Annual Review of Anthropology, 31*, 69–97.

Skutnabb-Kangas, T. (2007). Linguistic human rights in education? In O. Garcia & C. Baker, *Bilingual education: An introductory reader*. Bilingual education and bilingualism, 61. Clevedon: Multilingual Matters.

Skutnabb-Kangas, T., & Phillipson, R. (1994). *Linguistic imperialism*. Elmsford, NY: Pergamon Press.

Smith, L. T. (1999). *Decolonizing methodologies: Research and indigenous peoples*. London: Zed Books.

Solorzano, D. G. & Yosso, T. J. (2002). Critical race methodology: Counter-storytelling as an analytical framework for education research. *Qualitative Inquiry, 8*(1), 23–44.

Spivak, G. C. (1988). Can the subaltern speak? In C. Nelson & L. Grossberg, *Marxism and the interpretation of culture*. Urbana: University of Illinois Press.

Street, B. (1985). *Literacy in theory and practice*. London: Cambridge University Press.

Thoryk, R., Roberts, P., & Battistone, A. (2001). Both emic and etic: A view of the world through the lens of an ugly duckling. In L. Rogers & B. Swadener (Eds.), *Semiotics and dis/ability: Interrogating categories of difference*. Albany, NY: State University of New York Press.

Tobin, J. J. (1997). *Making a place for pleasure in early childhood education*. New Haven: Yale University Press.

Tobin, J. J. (2000). *"Good guys don't wear hats": Children's talk about the media*. New York: Teachers College Press.

Torstenson-Ed, T. (2007). Children's life paths through preschool and school. *Childhood, 14*(1), 47–66.

Varenne, H., & McDermott, R. (Eds.), (1999). *Successful failure: The school America builds*. Boulder, CO: Westview Press.

Ware, L.P. (2002). A moral conversation of disability: Risking the personal in educational contexts. *Hypatia, 17*(3), 143–172.

Woodward, J. C. (1972). Implications for sociolinguistic research among the deaf. *Sign Studies, 1*, 1–7.

Wortham, S. E. F. (2006). *Learning identity: The joint emergence of social identification and academic learning.* Cambridge: Cambridge University Press.

Wright, D. (1994). *Deafness: An autobiography.* New York: Harper Perennial.

Zizek, S. (1992). *Looking awry: An introduction to Jacques Lacan through popular culture.* Cambridge, MA: MIT Press.